NO

STRESS IN TEACHING

STRESS IN TEACHING

JACK DUNHAM

CROOM HELM
London & Sydney

NICHOLS PUBLISHING COMPANY
New York

© 1984 Jack Dunham
Croom Helm Ltd, Provident House, Burrell Row,
Beckenham, Kent BR3 1AT
Croom Helm Australia Pty Ltd, First Floor, 139 King Street,
Sydney, NSW 2001, Australia

British Library Cataloguing in Publication Data

Dunham, Jack
    Stress in teaching.
    1. Teachers — Great Britain — Job stress
    I. Title
    371.1'04   LB2840.2
    ISBN 0-7099-0852-0

First published in the United States of America 1982
by Nichols Publishing Company, Post Office Box 96, New York,
NY 10024

Library of Congress Cataloging in Publication Data

Dunham, Jack
    Stress in teaching.
    Bibliography: p. 171
    Includes index.
    1. Teachers — Job stress. 2. Teachers — Work load.
    I. Title
LB2840.2.D86 1984   371.1'001'9   84-8210
ISBN 0-89397-198-7

Printed and bound in Great Britain by
Biddles Ltd, Guildford and King's Lynn

CONTENTS

ACKNOWLEDGEMENTS

Stress in Teaching could not have been completed without the strong support of H.M.S., W.S., R.W.D., M.J.D., A.D.J., D.M.D., M.J., T.G.W. and J.A.W.

1 INTRODUCTION

The first step in tackling stress is to acknowledge its existence in teaching. Acceptance is difficult for people who associate stress with personal weakness and professional incompetence. For them admitting to classroom difficulties is paramount to admitting that they are bad teachers. They are afraid to disclose professional problems to colleagues who would regard them as signs of failure. They are unwilling to ask for help because that action would be seen as a form of weakness. Some of these barriers to stress reduction were identified by a teacher in a school for maladjusted children in a report to me in preparation for a staff conference:

> Stress is caused because I am unable to ask for extra support because if I did I would be assessed as a weak teacher by the rest of the staff.

The second step is to be clear about what the term stress means because several definitions are used by teachers. This issue of meaning is important because we need to know which definition teachers are using when they accept or deny the existence of stress.

There are three major approaches to understanding the nature of stress in teaching. The first approach looks at the pressures exerted on teachers in schools. A parallel is drawn with Hooke's Law of Electricity, the main elements of which are that of 'stress' — the load or demand which is placed on metal, and that of 'strain' — the deformation that results. The law states that if the strain produced by a given stress falls within the 'elastic limit' of the material, when the stress is removed the material will simply return to its original condition. If, however, the strain passes beyond the 'elastic limit', then some permanent damage will result. This model suggests that people, too, have their limits. Up to a point, stress can be tolerated, but when it becomes intolerable, damage may result, either psychological or physiological, or both. From this perspective stress 'is a set of causes, not a set of symptoms' (Symonds 1947). This is still a widely held view and is the basis of the argument that only certain groups of teachers, e.g. probationers, need programmes of guidance and support.

This engineering model equating external pressures with stress can be criticised on a number of grounds. There are wide individual differences

1

among teachers in their reactions to their first year of service, reorganisation, redeployment or other pressures. Some of them report stimulation rather than stress during these experiences. The extent to which the work demands made upon a teacher result in stress depends on a number of factors including pressures from sources external to teaching, personality and previous experience of similar demands.

The second approach to understanding stress is concerned with teachers' reactions to these pressures which consist of emotional and bodily manifestations such as headache, muscular tension and stomach ailments. From this perspective stress is defined as 'an unpleasant emotional state (e.g. tension, frustration, anxiety, emotional exhaustion)' (Kyriacou 1981). This view defines the concept of stress in terms of the degree that a person is experiencing persistent and high levels of anxiety or tension, which are identified in symptoms such as 'agitated', 'depressed', 'irritable', 'weepy', 'like a wet rag', 'can't concentrate', 'very tense' and 'can't switch off'. This perspective is illustrated in a letter I received in 1983:

> I should like to ask you a few questions concerning a friend of mine who has been teaching in a comprehensive school for four years. At the same time she has had fairly massive domestic problems. Since the second week of term she has been on sick leave. Her symptoms are persistent nausea, bouts of panic with very rapid heart-beats, sleeplessness, terrible feelings of panic and a tingling sensation in her limbs. Her doctor is treating her for stress but what I really wanted to ask you was:
> 1. Are these typical symptoms of stress?
> 2. How long do they take to be cured?
> 3. Does the cure involve leaving the teaching profession?
> 4. Are the symptoms if cured for the moment likely to recur?

These questions bring out the strong medical orientation of this approach to understanding stress which is one of its major weaknesses. There are important manifestations which are not emotional or psychosomatic and so tend to be ignored by people using this definition. A Head of Department expressed one difficulty during an in-service training course:

> The awareness of stress is an important issue. Many people seem unable to recognise the signs in themselves or feel that they are letting themselves down if they admit to stress.

One significant type of problem which is frequently not defined as stress-related is ineffectiveness in the performance of one's role in school. The experience of becoming ineffective is often identified by a major loss of confidence and is particularly worrying to staff who have been competent and confident for a number of years. Some of the consequences of a reduction in effort and competence because of an increase in stress were set out very clearly by a Head of Department in a preparatory report to me for a stress reduction workshop:

> I tried hard to forget school during the vacation and I refused for the first time in 10 years to spend time in the classroom before the holiday was over. I did not finish my aims and obligations for which the Head has been waiting for a long time. I tried to accept that my time and talent were limited but I find it very hard. I have still not decorated the classroom and I have used more available and less original material in my lessons. For the first time I have re-issued notes from previous years.

The third approach to explaining stress is concerned with both pressures and reactions and also the coping resources which teachers use as they attempt to cope with their difficulties. Stress from this perspective means a significant excess of pressures over coping resources. This interactionist approach emphasises the importance of identifying the demands which teachers perceive and experience as stressful and the behaviour they use to tackle these demands. Coping behaviour has been defined by Mechanic (1967) as 'the application of a person's acquired skills, techniques and knowledge' and he has argued that in attempting to understand stress more attention should be given to problem solving and coping behaviour.

This view proposes that the extent to which a teacher experiences stress in any situation in school depends upon a number of factors which include: appraisal of demands and his or her strategies to deal with them; anticipation of likely future demanding experiences and his or her state of readiness to tackle them; the extent of the preparation and rehearsal of the skills necessary for the teacher to handle work pressures effectively.

I use the interactionist model as the basis of my in-service training in stress reduction skills and it will be used as a framework for this book. My definition of stress is: a process of behavioural, emotional, mental and physical reactions caused by prolonged, increasing or new pressures which are significantly greater than coping resources. The plan of the book follows the three parts of the definition: Chapters Two, Three, Four and Five are concerned with helping teachers in primary and secondary schools to become more aware of the pressures which are experienced by their colleagues so that they can be encouraged to identify their own pressures; Chapter Six is related to the demands on Headteachers and Deputy Heads and Chapter Seven discusses the heavy loads experienced by Heads of Department and House and Year Heads; Chapter Eight reports the stress reactions of all staff and Chapter Nine records the different strategies which staff use as they tackle their pressures and reactions; in Chapters Ten and Eleven I offer a number of recommendations for strengthening coping resources.

All the subsequent chapters use information which I have been given by staff in my action research projects in courses and conferences in schools, colleges, teachers' centres and universities. The research is an integral part of the awareness and skills training. I ask for information before a course or conference about the members' pressures, reactions, resources and recommendations for the reduction of stress. This is summarised and reported back when I participate in the session. If it is a school-based staff conference I visit the school and interview some staff before the conference — during which I report back my information and also suggest a framework for a stress reduction programme for staff. Reporting back is an essential test of the accuracy of my perception of how they are dealing with the sources of stress in school. A follow-up session to review the effectiveness of the stress reduction programme after about six months is gradually becoming more accepted by teachers as a necessary part of my work.

I have collected written and oral information from about 1,350 teachers including Heads, Deputies and Heads of Department, and House and Year Heads. Much of it is presented in this book which I see as another form of feedback to be tested for its accuracy by teachers individually and in groups. A considerable amount of information is presented in the words of the teachers themselves so that their colleagues in the profession can share these experiences of stress, learn from their attempts to reduce it and, perhaps most importantly, end their feelings of suffering from stress in isolation. In this book, as in my in-service training, I see myself as a facilitator and not as an 'expert' and I offer it with thanks.

2 STAFF PROBLEMS CAUSED BY ORGANISATIONAL AND CURRICULAR CHANGES

This chapter investigates the major changes teachers have experienced in the last decade which have altered their schools and the work they do in the classrooms. These changes have included the demands of reorganisation and the development of schemes of pastoral care for those pupils with personal and family problems. At the present time, staff are under pressure to use new and more rigorous methods for the appraisal of their work and to maintain high professional standards in the face of reduced financial support in schools.

For the majority of teachers, reorganisation originally meant the organisational and curricular changes which were required to implement their LEAs policy for comprehensive education. This earlier reorganisation was associated with growth and was very different from contemporary developments which are usually based on contraction.

For some teachers the establishment of comprehensive schools had a very positive meaning. They felt, as one of the teachers expressed it to me:

A sense of relief and a sense of not being bottled up, even of liberation.

These teachers perceived new opportunities for fresh patterns of teaching; new relationships; new patterns of involvement in worthwhile developments; fresh opportunities for personal and professional growth; and better prospects for promotion.

But for some of their colleagues the process of moving from a secondary modern or grammar school into a comprehensive school created several adjustments which seemed to have four major aspects (Dunham 1976):

(i) leaving the security of a familiar environment in the previous school;
(ii) working in larger and more complex schools;
(iii) teaching pupils who had a much wider range of abilities, behaviour and attitudes;

(iv)   adapting to major organisational and curricular changes.

Some of these changes were perceived before reorganisation as threats and were viewed with apprehension. During my discussions with teachers about the adjustments they would have to make to achieve a successful transition to the comprehensive system in their LEA a number of worries were expressed. Staff were concerned about the differences between their present pupils and those in the new school. They were apprehensive about the problems of discipline they might encounter. They thought that they would have to modify their own patterns of behaviour to which they had become accustomed over a number of years. These familiar routines and rituals had given them security because there were so few unexpected demands. Unfortunately the limitations of a narrow range of school experience made them vulnerable to the uprooting aspect of reorganisation.

The significance of this kind of vulnerability can be seen in the experience of a teacher who had been working in a new purpose-built comprehensive school for about a year. She told me that she was experiencing much less job satisfaction in her present school than in the small country grammar school which had been her only post and in which she had worked for ten years. Reorganisation had brought several losses: she and her colleagues were required to leave the old grammar school buildings and to move into new buildings on a new site. She also left behind her Headmaster who chose the time of reorganisation to retire. He had ruled the school as a benevolent and autocratic father-figure for over 20 years. The man appointed to take his place seemed inadequate to her because he was not satisfying her needs for recognition and support. She said she was not adapting very well to these changes and that she was depressed. She seemed to be suffering from grief for the loss of the grammar school and of the kind of working life it had meant for her.

But reorganisation meant more than trying to come to terms with personal losses. It was necessary for staff to attempt to cope with the differences in the new school. For many teachers this meant working in a much larger school and for them this was one of the most severe demands they encountered.

The process of adaptation to a larger school has been perceptively analysed by the Head of an Avon secondary school (Hinton 1974). Many teachers confuse the problems of comprehensive reorganisation with those of size. Most of us are simply unused to very large schools. We went to smaller schools; we taught in smaller schools. It is a slow and uneasy process adjusting to what is not just a smaller school writ large, but a different kind of institution in all sorts of significant ways.

One of the important differences Hinton identified was the difficulty of developing a sense of belonging to a big organisation. In the largest schools there was a considerable risk that the organisation would be perceived as so impersonal and so fragmented that a sense of common purpose would be very difficult to achieve. In these circumstances it became difficult to find points of identification with staff and pupils. For teachers who had served in small schools where they felt the satisfaction of shared aims the demands involved in these changes presented severe problems. These large schools were also much more complex organisations which included split-site working, complicated disciplinary procedures, impersonal communication systems instead of the face-to-face contact of previous schools and new administrative structures which included executive teams, policy and planning committees and staff working parties.

Teachers going into comprehensive schools were also required to adjust to a different intake of pupils who had a much wider range of behaviour, abilities and attitudes. A minority of these pupils had learning, disciplinary and emotional problems which were outside the training and experience of their teachers. Some long-serving members of staff, with the limited experience which made them vulnerable to change, had a demoralising awareness of incompetence and loss of confidence for the first time for many years. They were surprised and occasionally shocked at the behaviour and language of their pupils. One teacher reported:

> It is not the physical aspects which cause difficulty, as these are not too extreme, so much as the psychological battering one receives to one's ego; for example one's requests being ignored and the verbal abuse.

These teachers were also disturbed by the intensity of their own emotional reactions in classroom, corridor and staffroom. Their previous teaching had not aroused their emotions so strongly: they had simulated anger for disciplinary purposes — now they were really angry: they had believed that teaching was like playing a dramatic role on the stage (Casey 1976), now their own attitudes, values and skills were being tested to the full.

These demands were compounded in a number of schools by major organisational and curricular changes. These pressures have been clearly identified by the Head of the Avon secondary school I quoted earlier in this chapter:

> When schools go comprehensive teachers are thrust into a variety of quite unfamiliar teaching and pastoral situations. They have to cope with children of both sexes, all ages and abilities, with a plethora of new methods and curricula, and with changing attitudes and standards which often seem to devalue skills and philosophies in which they have a heavy emotional investment. They have to adjust to a large number of new colleagues in the immediate aftermath of the anxiety and disturbance, which reorganisation inevitably brings.

These possible sources of stress, which the Head has identified, were not staggered to give teachers the opportunity of adjusting to one major change before having to cope with the next one. In the schools where all the problems associated with secondary school reorganisation were experienced by staff almost simultaneously, resistance to present and further changes became a self-protective strategy. It was clearly expressed in a Staff report which was discussed at a secondary school staff development conference in which I participated:

> We felt that when this school was opened we were thrown into far too much change. There were too many ideas that we were trying to operate all at the same time and this gave us a great deal of insecurity. We lacked stability. We had far too many things that we could not cope with and this was the root cause of our trouble. We felt that it was not too late to impose some stability, to stop the changes, to keep going as we are and build slowly on what we have got. We want to improve the quality of life for the children in the school but we cannot do this when we are developing too rapidly to give ourselves a secure base from which to work.

One of the early innovations in this school as in other comprehensive schools was mixed ability teaching (MAT). When I visited the school to interview staff and prepare for their staff development conference, it was apparent that a considerable number of teachers were experiencing difficulties as a consequence of teaching unstreamed classes of pupils with very different attainments in the basic subjects. The Headteacher had circulated a questionnaire to assess their opinions about teaching unstreamed attainment groups. In their replies Staff indicated their feelings of worry and inadequacy. One teacher wrote:

I lack personal experience of M.A.T. as I do not teach the first and second years but the casual comments of my colleagues are discouraging. I am very worried at the dilution of the academic content of the school and the bland assumption that mixing will somehow raise the morale of the less able but not work conversely with the more able.

One of her colleagues expressed her feelings much more briefly:

I am not qualified nor able to cope with MA teaching.

These pressures on teachers arising from the change to working with unstreamed groups have been reported by other writers, one of whom concluded, after a major study of organisational and curricular changes in a comprehensive school:

Once the problem of looking critically at teaching methods is faced, teachers find themselves having to embark on the painful process of reassessing their own skills, perhaps after years of successful teaching (Richardson 1973).

These pressures arising from the many different kinds of changes involved in secondary school reorganisation, have not come to an end. There are schemes being submitted to the Secretary of State and decisions are being taken about them which will have major consequences for the teachers concerned. Details of a current problem were given to me in November 1982 by the Deputy Head of a grammar school:

The problem I am likely to be faced with in the near future is concerned with secondary reorganisation. This has been impending for the last twenty years but a decision seems possible later this year. The scheme before the Secretary of State involves converting this school into a Sixth Form College. The problem for the staff will be that although all of them with a couple of exceptions want to be in the Sixth Form College, it is unlikely that more than 50% will be. However the reorganisation proposals require all the staff, whether they have a future in the Sixth Form College or not, to work in the dwindling Grammar School during the interim period of around four years. Early retirement will not be an option as we have virtually no staff over 45 and their chances of being employed in other similar schools to ours are naturally very limited. A new Head starts next term. How do I minimise the stress and loss of morale to those staff who do not get jobs in the Sixth Form College but have to stay in the Grammar School for as long as it exists? I suppose it's a common problem, but not one that is in my experience.

Another secondary school in the same LEA is also facing major changes which were identified by the Head in a letter inviting me to take part in a staff in-service training day:

This school is a three form entry girls secondary modern school. At present the roll stands at 500 but this will soon drop to approximately 465. There are 30 members of staff including myself. I believe that my staff, in common with those in other schools, are under considerable pressure at the moment with falling rolls and the prospect of reorganisation of the city schools in a year's time. I shall be grateful therefore if you can air this problem and give us some guidance in coping with it as a staff.

The reorganisation which these teachers will encounter very shortly will be a merger with another secondary school in the city. This will create several changes for the staff of both schools but one of the most important will be alterations in the roles of those teachers with management responsibilities: Headteachers, Deputies, Heads of Department and Heads of House and Year. It is highly unlikely that job-sharing will be introduced by this LEA. What is much more probable is that there will be a reduction in the status, prestige and job satisfaction for those members of staff not appointed to their previous levels of responsibility in the new school. An indication of the possible effects of these changes was contained in a letter sent to me in March 1983 by a Head of Department shortly before one of my courses for middle management. He wrote:

My main source of stress in my present post has been brought about by the following situation — I am Head of Department in a 'new' school brought about by a merger. In the department there are also two other teachers who have been Head of Department in the 'old' school, which now houses the new school. It has been difficult on occasions to introduce new ideas and changes without causing upset and I have been extremely aware of the anxiety and stress for all concerned. I have tried to overcome certain situations by taking on jobs myself and therefore lessening the stress situation. Making decisions without consultation with the others has helped as it lessens any conflict situation which we all politely try to avoid. Sometimes I switch off completely and adopt an action which takes me right away from it all — playing squash is one way for me.

The teachers in this school who were not appointed to the Head of Department positions are also being affected by another major change. Earlier in their careers, if this problem had occurred, they would have sought and probably obtained a similar post or gained promotion in another school. But at the present time these opportunities are more restricted, and they are likely to feel that further promotion either inside or outside their school is improbable. This has resulted in some instances in the development of feelings of being 'trapped'. The problem is not restricted to Heads of Department and an indication of the meaning of contraction for other teachers is contained in the report of a Deputy Head:

> The Houghton awards and the consequent reduction in teaching scales have meant that large numbers of teachers on Scales 2 and 3 are unable to gain further promotion. This in itself has led to a certain discontentment among staff, which affects their relations with the hierarchy, but add to this the fact that discretionary posts are not being re-filled when they fall vacant (due to educational cuts) and you have a worsening situation in which the workload of 3rd Deputies and Senior Teachers may well be shared among teachers who already feel frustrated at their inability to gain promotion.

This major change from expansion to contraction in the Education Service as a whole and in the career prospects of teachers has also been strongly felt in primary schools where the growth of urgent financial problems is accelerating. These cuts in educational expenditure are producing a continually changing pattern of economies which impose serious pressures. These include reductions in staffing at all levels; a virtually complete embargo on all appointments — even of replacements; the restriction of building repairs and maintenance; reductions in support provision such as the School Psychological Service and the Remedial Education Service; capitation allowances are frozen at a fraction of the previous year's allowance; and reductions in meal-time staffing are increasing.

Some of the increasing pressures arising from these cuts on the Heads and teachers in the primary schools of one LEA were reported by the Headteachers:

(i)   Reduction in part-time teaching staff so Head has more teaching time.

(ii)   Reduction in secretarial hours so Head has less help to deal with administration (which is increasing).

(iii)   Reduction in School Meal allowances so that meals sent to school leave no room for flexibility resulting in stress to school meals staff and Head.

(iv)   Total cut of remedial assistance which means that the staff have to give a lot more time to certain children at the expense of others.

(v)   Teachers have to spend more hours in school talking, preparing, etc.

(vi)   Teachers have to make do with limited resources and so share books between children or do group work because of it. The class organisation and curriculum are governed by the available resources not what the teacher thinks is the best method of working.

(vii)   Less mobility in teaching profession so there are fewer opportunities for promotion.

Two other important problems have been identified. They are staff allocation and redeployment. The possible sources of stress in each of these situations have been clearly presented by a Head in another LEA. For the last five years his school has suffered falling rolls which, together with the cuts in public spending, led to a reduced staffing allocation for the school, but he was invited by his Education Officer to make out a case for extra staff for 'curriculum support'. The Head also arranged to hold special meetings of governors and parents, and petitions and letters were sent to Councillors and the Education Committee to back up his requests for extra staff. The sources of stress in this situation for the Head were:

(1)   The 'here we go again' feeling. There was resentment at the time and effort involved in struggling to retain the *status quo* rather than working to improve things. A slow erosion of morale resulted from this for all the staff.

(2)   Anxiety over what would happen if there were no 'reprieve',

because it was emphasised by the Education Officer at a
governor's meeting that there would be no reprieve this time.
This would have meant classes of up to 35 in small classrooms
and would have drastically undermined the basis of the school
with its emphasis on the development of the individual child.
(There was a reprieve.)

(3)   The time and effort involved in writing reports, collecting
information about details of special needs, etc., holding meetings with governors and parents, writing letters to Councillors.

(4)   Poor relationships with the Education Office personnel. The
uncertainty seemed to lead to a sort of paranoia, when nobody
was trusted.

The redeployment problem for this Head occurred in 1982. It arose
in the summer term when the Education Officer decided to advertise
for only two of the three vacancies and to leave the third one open for
the possible redeployment of a teacher. The decision was taken after
the final date for serving teachers to give notice of resignation so the
applications were restricted to probationers and temporary staff (over
300 applied). Two teachers were appointed. A teacher who had been
nominated for redeployment was sent to the school to be interviewed
for the vacancy. She was well qualified; she had also recently changed
schools twice. After meeting her the Head and the staff decided they
could not accept her as a colleague. The teacher was 'passed on' to
another school. It was now near the end of the summer term and to the
Head it seemed like a 'war of nerves' between the Education Office
administrators and the school. Finally, two weeks before the end of the
term, the Education Officer told the Head that he could appoint his
choice. One of the short-listed applicants for the two other posts was
still available and was appointed.

The Head did not learn much about the feelings of the redeployed
teacher who was not appointed. He said she shared his embarrassment.
There is a possibility of more serious consequences for redeployed
teachers, some of which can be noted in my interview with a teacher
in an infants school. She contacted me shortly after the end of the
summer term. I went to interview her at her home and I asked her to
write a record of the major events of the last two weeks of the term.
Her report starts with the staff being told that the school had to lose
one teacher:

Friday, 6th July
There was a Staff Meeting to discuss the redeployment of a teacher.
Our Adviser came to tell us, the whole staff both Junior and Infant
teachers, that at the end of term one of the full-time teachers would
have to go. After a general discussion, with vague facts, and points
raised by only a few of the staff, i.e. the Deputy Head, the Head of
Infants, *myself* and one other, we were invited to have individual
interviews with the Adviser, the Headmaster also being present. Half
of the staff stayed on for these interviews (it being 5.30) and the
rest were to have interviews on Monday. I had my interview on
Friday; three main questions were asked: age, mobility, dependants.
Various other points may have been raised, but the interview was
fairly relaxed but one felt almost fatalistic about it. (All the staff
came out of the interview feeling it was going to be them!)
Monday, 9th July
We all knew the Adviser was coming; there was therefore obvious
concern which appeared to be felt by everyone and his possible
arrival was a constant topic of conversation. He must have arrived in
the middle of the afternoon, because at 3.20 I was summoned by the
Headmaster to see him again. There was a sinking feeling and an
instant realisation that it was going to be me! The interview was even
in the same room as the interviews for Redeployment held in 1977.
The Adviser told me immediately he was asking me to be redeployed. My immediate reaction was '*Why me!*' He hummed and
haa'd for a bit and then said I was experienced and I was possibly
the 'best' one, i.e. adaptable. I cannot remember the exact words.
I was naturally upset but able to cope with the situation. As the
Headmaster was not present, I felt able to talk openly, and I men-
tioned tactfully and briefly that I had been almost redeployed
before. I wanted to find out if possible if the Headmaster had been
involved in the choice. The Adviser said not — and I suppose I
wanted to agree with him — he had been seen to be very fair — and
now was being very understanding and as helpful as possible in the
circumstances. After a long discussion, we then went into the Headmaster's office. I did go into the staffroom briefly — to find the
Deputy Head and a junior teacher who had waited behind to see me.
The rest of the staff had gone home previously. The Adviser was
obviously anxious to go — he said he had to go and see a junior
Headmaster — did I want to go with him? A junior post? Certainly
not I said — I am a fully qualified and experienced infant teacher.
The Headmaster gave me a lift home. Then followed a night of

telephone calls and no sleep (I dropped off between 3 and 5), waking early, exhausted and *very* agitated and concerned. During the night my main feeling was one of intense anger and frustration and panic?

Friday, 20th July

My last teaching day at the school was spent clearing up, completing some records — and organising my own boxes of equipment. The lunch time celebrations in the Staffroom proved to be quite light-hearted (there were 3 teachers leaving) — and I had a sad and very touching farewell from my children, and especially my parents — those I know well came in to give me a beautiful present, a bouquet and make their goodbyes.

Monday, 23rd July

I went into school to complete my packing and leave my boxes in the corridor. The infant teacher who was taking over my room was in the process together with the Head of Infants, of dismantling the shelf areas and completely changing the whole room. I must admit I felt as though it was an acknowledgement of how little I had achieved. I know it wasn't, but it did leave me feeling rather lost and inadequate.

Wednesday, 25th July

Now I have to do all my records of attainments, etc. in the holidays. Unfortunately I always like to do them thoroughly and before the end of term — usually in the last two weeks. But this has been no ordinary end of term for me. The records will be done in the holiday, as thoroughly as the circumstances will permit. Half of me feels why should I bother? But this is not the way I work and I will attempt to do the work to the best of my ability, e.g. the social/emotional records, the attainment records of Maths and Reading/Writing (all personal to the school) and the new Mathematics and Literacy Records, of which the latter require the presence of the children. But as I said before this is not an ordinary end of term, or for that matter the usual beginning to the summer holiday.

The effect of redeployment on the school as a whole should also be considered, because the pressures may affect more people than is at first apparent. This was the firm conclusion of the Deputy Head of a secondary school who presented several important issues in her report:

We have experienced serious problems when going through the redeployment procedure. They are:

(i) The effects on the identified staff which are mainly emotional and traumatic and which are reflected on to their families; they feel that they have been rejected by their school; they feel that they are no good and that they have no future in the profession.

(ii) The effects on the colleagues of the identified staff in the staff-room which appear to be mainly feelings of guilt and uncertainty about how to react.

(iii) The relationships between the identified staff and senior colleagues have become very fragile and in some cases they have been destroyed.

(iv) The role of the LEA staff is very important; they should not consult with the Headteacher and the Deputies in identifying the member of staff and then withdraw leaving the school to pick up the pieces; this is most important for it is not sufficient just to encourage the teacher to apply for suitable jobs — they require much more guidance.

(v) The role of union representatives can be very tricky but they have a crucial part to play.

The leaving part of the redeployment process, which is discussed in my interview and in this report, may not be the most difficult part of these changes. Adjusting to a new school in these circumstances can bring heavy pressures. This appeared to be the experience of five redeployed teachers who talked about some of their problems:

I felt that the Head had been forced to accept me.

I felt that I had been forced to accept the job.

I felt that my colleagues regarded me with suspicion.

I think the Head resents having to appoint me.

I think a redeployed teacher is a kind of stigma.

These five teachers had been redeployed because their school was closing at the end of the school year. School closures will continue to put a number of teachers 'at risk' in relation to stress (Dunham 1982), but there are probably more staff experiencing heavy demands because of the threat of school closure. Some of these pressures were identified by the Head of a primary school whose school had been visited by the

County Council Falling Rolls Panel in the previous year. After this visit the Panel proposed that his school should be closed as part of a reorganisation plan for the area. The stress caused by this proposal was considerable on everyone in the school and at my invitation he analysed the stress situations which he had experienced:

(1) Extra Paper Work: Obviously I am heavily committed to the opposition of these proposals, and this has involved me in a considerable amount of extra paper work which includes —
a. Preparation of school dossier.
b. Research and preparation of a document which gave the arguments for the survival of the school.
c. Increase in Reports to Governors (average of 3 Governors meetings per term). This, in a way, has been a good exercise in that it helps one reappraise one's values and principles in education.
(2) Press/TV/Radio: Both local and national press and TV (plus Schools Radio) have taken an interest in our case, and this has led to a considerable amount of time and 'stress energy' being spent on press interviews, etc.
(3) 'Spreading the Word': I have found it particularly stressful to repeat the arguments of our case over and over again to a variety of people in all walks of life. It is important to do this to gain the support we need, but changing one's language style to suit the type of listener (i.e. not being too technical to the non-professional, yet presenting a clear and reasoned argument) is a type of stress that seems unnoticeable at first, but would appear to have a cumulative effect as time goes on.
(4) The Parents: Although I have enjoyed considerable support from the parents, and this is a valuable resource, it has been paid for with a lot of diplomacy! This includes taking time to talk to individuals, making sure they are kept informed of developments and organising meetings in the evenings.
(5) Governors: Again, these have been a source of support, but the extra liaison needed over the fight to save the School has caused extra worry and time consumption.
(6) Time: All these demands involve spending a lot of time on extra work. As a 'teaching head' this has meant less time with my family and although they understand the problems and have given me a lot of support it has caused tension at home.
(7) The stress factor has been considerable during the past year

because of the Falling Rolls Panel's proposals which were added to the normal pressures of everyday teaching.

The ordinary demands of primary school teaching to which this Head refers have also increased in recent years. They include team teaching; the use of modern teaching methods which emphasise the importance of individual children's needs; the rapid expansion of the curriculum to include science, drama, new forms of craft, dance, 'new' mathematics and computers; the expansion of out-of-school activities; the requirements of new legislation; fêtes, competitions and sales to raise funds for the school.

The changes in primary and secondary schools have not been properly assimilated and a moratorium of five years to give teachers the opportunity to come to terms with recent and current innovations would seem to be a reasonable conclusion to this chapter. It would also be unrealistic because it is possible to identify the emergence of new pressures; these include the use of assessment procedures for Heads, teachers, departments, pastoral care units and schools and the participation by parents in the work and management of schools.

Staff will be asked to integrate these developments into their professional practice while they are still working through unresolved problems. The next chapter examines one of the most severe of these continuing difficulties — role conflict.

3 THE PROBLEMS OF ROLE CONFLICT AND ROLE AMBIGUITY

In this chapter I shall support the argument that role conflict and role ambiguity are major sources of stress for staff as, for example, when teachers also have pastoral care responsibilities as tutors. These demands lead to stress when they clash: a girl wants to talk to her tutor about a personal problem (a suspected pregnancy) when he is on his way to teach his VIth Form physics class. Role conflict is also experienced because an increasing number of expectations are being directed on to teachers from parents, the media, LEAs and HMIs.

Role Conflict – Contradictory Expectations

Two types of role conflict will be identified. The first arises because of contradictory expectations, for example the Deputy Head may be the 'person in the middle' between his Headmaster who may want to initiate changes and his colleagues in the staffroom, who are resisting them. Role conflict also occurs when parental expectations of pupil achievement, behaviour and attitudes are in conflict with staff expectations and the Head becomes the fulcrum for these opposing pressures, doing a precarious balancing act in the middle of the seesaw. Teachers may experience very different expectations of what their role should be, e.g. language teachers are confronted with markedly distinct interpretations of their job and the tension between these demands causes stress (Burke and Dunham 1982). Staff may have seasonal periods of increased pressures and conflict, e.g. music teachers when they are heavily involved in the preparation and performance of Christmas music.

The demands on Heads which can lead to this first type of role conflict can be illustrated by two analyses of their roles. The first, presented in Figure 3.1, summarises the expectations which secondary school Heads face from many different sources. The second, presented in Figure 3.2, was completed by the Head of a small primary school who had kept a record of all his face-to-face contacts during the previous school year (Luke 1980).

These patterns of demands become more meaningful with the

Figure 3.1: Headteachers' Role Demands in Secondary Schools

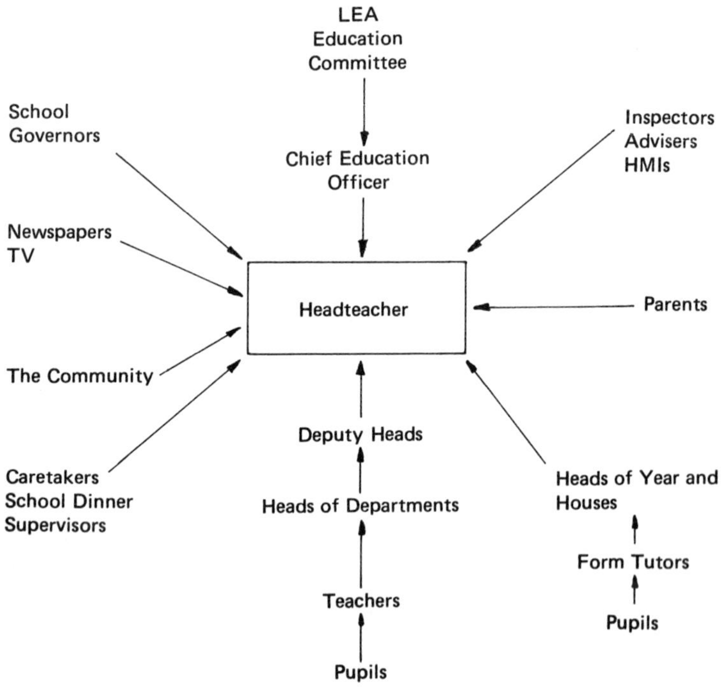

presentation of Heads' reports of their role conflict. The following reports, of the Heads of four different types of schools, are used as examples of this type of conflict. The Head of a secondary school identified a wide range of pressures:

> The Head is at the centre of all the internal and external transactions of the school with the consequent need to make rapid adjustments when dealing with pupils, colleagues, governors, parents, meals staff, and in my case a range of building contractors working on the site of this new school.

The Head of an infants' school on the other hand experienced stress from demand and disturbing pressures which were exerted on her from a parent and her LEA:

> In my previous school when I was a fairly new Head, I received a confidential letter from my County Education Officer stating that

Figure 3.2: A Headteacher's Role Demands in a Primary School

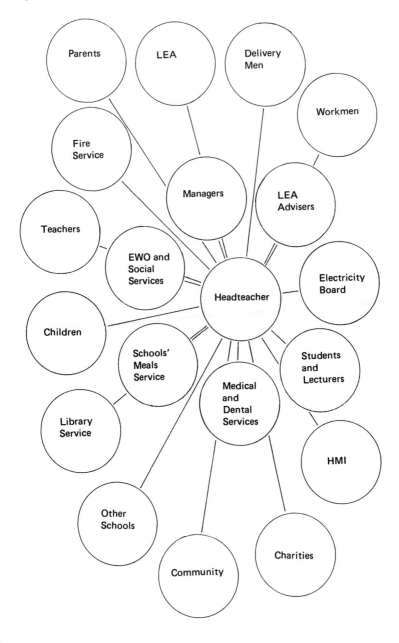

the LEA had received a letter of complaint from a parent over an incident which was supposed to have occurred in the dining room – my 'force feeding' of a small child. I was asked to give my side of the story. My response to this was to phone the county office, as I could not recall this particular incident. The stress was aggravated when I was told to put my reply in writing and was also recommended to contact my professional organisation. This left me feeling that the LEA believed the accusation made against me and did not intend to help me. Now with more experience I realise that such things happen to Headteachers, some time in their life. I would recommend more publicity to potential Headteachers, to inform them that these things do happen to those in authority.

The Headteacher of a middle school described his role as that of an intermediary between various interests, lobbies and disputants. He reported that the most frequent stress situations are those involving different sections of staff (teaching, cleaning, kitchen, secretarial) and parents. Those directly involving pupils seem to be more clear cut. His greatest difficulty was concerned with situations in which a member of staff seems justifiably criticised by pupils or parents. The conflict of the Headmistress of a small primary school was concerned with the demands of parents, teachers, pupils and administration. She was the first Head of a new school on an estate, with Council and National Coal Board houses. The whole estate to the Head seemed 'anti-everything, especially anti authority'. There were four working areas in the school (117 on roll) with the Head as a teaching Head, and three young teachers, one with two years' experience and the other two in their probationary year. The pressures of keeping these young members of staff from the irate attentions of various parents and coping with a class and the administration proved too much in the end for the Head. She became ill, applied for another appointment and got it. The staff left with her.

Deputy Heads are also subject to conflict because of contradictory expectations (Open University 1976). This is experienced when they attempt to resolve the demands of day-to-day work and the need for long-term planning, i.e. between the tactical and the strategic; between the minutiae and the helicopter-view. They are also exposed to expectations from different sources which often appear to be difficult to integrate. Deputies may be expected by the staff to 'belong' in the staffroom and to identify with and conform to staff norms. They may be expected by the Head to identify with his aims and his decisions rather than support the staff. These aspects of pressures on Deputies can be seen in the following letter from the Deputy Head of a secondary school:

> The main source of stress for me is lack of time – a list of things to be done which never gets shorter! When I first became a deputy I was very aware of the fact that the job is very vague – I was not sure what I had to do, and I felt that the staff were ready to criticise if I was not being continually active. Now, however, my main sources of stress are in dealing with the continual role of peacemaker. Everybody brings you their point of view – often about the action of the head or other members of staff leaving the deputy no safety valve. The other difficulty is when my views differ from the head. I find it impossible to present views to the staff as if I agree with them, when I don't. I would prefer to be able to be open about different opinions – but have to take refuge in silence as the Head considers we should not have different views as far as the staff are concerned.

The role conflict of the Deputy's job can also be identified in the report of a Deputy Head of a primary school who described the stress which she experienced after the appointment of a new Head:

> He was 10 years younger than me and had no experience of working with Infant or Lower Junior age children. At first the staff were welcoming but gradually tired of watching what they considered unwise decisions. Many of the staff were very experienced teachers and resentment grew. I was often asked to voice their dissent and this put me in a very difficult situation.

Heads of Department may also experience this kind of role conflict when they act as intermediaries between their own department and other departments in the school or with the pastoral care heads of houses and years (Marland 1971). The Head of Department is thus required to act as a negotiator pressing the claims of the members of his department and defending their arguments. He may find that other Heads of Department and the Pastoral Heads are very sensitive when they think that anyone is encroaching on their particular areas of responsibility. Conflict may also be experienced with pastoral care staff, e.g. Head of Department may have to go through a pastoral care intermediary to contact parents and the intermediary is a junior member of the Head of Department's department.

The Head of Department is also the link between the teachers in his department and the Head. The former may perceive his function to be to put their point of view to the Head, while the latter may perceive the Head of Department's role to have an important controlling function. These different perspectives and expectations with their potential for role conflict can be illustrated by the experience of a drama teacher in a comprehensive school. In her drama lessons she had been attempting to modify the unfavourable attitudes towards drama of twelve- and thirteen-year-old boys and girls by discussing their own experiences and then dramatising them. The pupils who had been very suspicious at the beginning of the school year were now beginning to express their thoughts and feelings more fluently. Most of the group said they enjoyed these lessons. The teacher knew that the pupils wanted to continue this approach to drama.

In her drama lessons in the hall the teacher was using unstructured situations, which involved the building of a precariously balanced impromptu scaffolding of tables and chairs. The Headmaster, passing by, saw this expression of 'creative drama' at its most exciting: the topmost part of the column was swaying, the children were considerably involved in the proceedings and the noise level was much higher than the norm for the school. At the end of the lesson the teacher was told by the Head that what he had seen was not 'drama'. It was he said, 'a group out of control'. The Head of the English department was given the same comment. She was in the first year of her appointment and she was working hard to initiate changes in the teaching approaches used by members of the department. She thought that the Head had agreed with her ideas when she was interviewed for her post. She had encouraged the young teacher to introduce the new techniques, but she now felt angry and disappointed by the Head's remarks because she was now the 'woman-in-the-middle', being pulled in different directions by these contradictory role expectations.

Role Conflict – Interaction Between Pupils, Teachers and Parents

Another source of role conflict for Heads of Department can be found in the interaction between pupils, teachers and parents. A clear example of this kind of problem was provided by a Head of Department who gave me a detailed analysis of his role conflict:

To me Mr. X seems incompetent: to the Adviser he is 'average'. He has failed on numerous occasions to supply marks, schemes of work, drafts of examinations, etc. He has constantly fallen behind on syllabuses, which makes life boring for the boys, without taking account of the deterioration in examination performance. He has been absent on flimsy excuses. He is late going to and leaving lessons. When he does take in work, it is returned eventually (three months is not rare) in a terrible state. The boys are painfully aware of the situation and the result is that they do not respect him and there is no successful working relationship — even the pupils think that he is too easy-going. Complaints have been received from parents. Colleagues have noted that he helps in no way with any of the out-of-school activities. Transfer would seem to be the answer but the Advsier does not think that this would be possible. The Headmaster and I have discussed the matter fully and have tried all we can, but quite simply we are the victims of circumstances, i.e. an inherited situation. I am worried because he teaches 40% of the subject in the school and the subject will not get off the ground as long as he remains. Finally, where do we put him? Next year he will be teaching all the 1st and 2nd year classes, and the bottom set of the 3rd, 4th and 5th forms, with only two periods with the 6th form, seeing that he finds it impossible to maintain intellectual discipline and meet syllabus deadlines in the 6th form.

Incompetent teachers like Mr. X increase the workload of Heads of Department to a significant degree. It is important, therefore, to note that there are now more opportunities than until quite recently to bring disciplinary proceedings against teachers whose professional performance is as unprofessional as that of Mr. X. Such proceedings can include dismissal (Barrell 1983). These actions may appear distasteful to some Heads of Department and even disloyal to the members of their department. There is, therefore, the possibility of a clash of loyalties involving an individual teacher who may have been a colleague for some years, the other members of the department who may be bearing increased workloads and, finally, the Head because of strong parental pressures. These conflicting demands which Heads of Department experience and which can make such a significant contribution to their stress also play a major part in the work pressures of the Pastoral Care Heads (Blackburn 1983). These Heads of House and Heads of Year are presented with disciplinary and pastoral problems which require their attention and decisions. These problems may be presented urgently for immediate response to what appear to be crisis situations. They may be brought to their attention in the staffroom or when they are going to their lessons because it appears to be common practice for Pastoral Care Heads to carry a major teaching responsibility. These problems are clearly identified in the following report:

> As a Head of House in a comprehensive school (14–18 years being the pupils' age range) I find one of the major stress situations occurs when important 'house business' has to be done when there is no real time to deal with it. Two days in the week especially seem to be more stressful than others. (a) Tuesday, our house duty day when I am responsible for organising staff and prefects' duties. I have two free periods but break times and lunch times are not really available for seeing pupils or colleagues. (b) Wednesday, when I teach every lesson, and the day starts with our house assembly, which I have responsibility for organising. Obviously things happen on these days which require urgent attention e.g. a pupil reported over a discipline matter, letters to write home, a reference or court report which needs to be written fairly urgently.
>
> One is faced with the decisions over dealing with the problems immediately, as soon as they come to light, and thus neglecting one's other duties e.g. teaching, or delaying dealing with the problems until time is available. Each solution, or the compromise which often results, brings some anxiety or stress.
>
> Feverish activity often results, lack of concentration and patience in lessons is also possible. In general I feel that classroom teaching must come first (as a general rule), thus one is left with problems to deal with 'as soon as possible' (this can result in things being rushed due to lack of time, or in a significant delay occurring before any action is taken).
>
> There would seem to be no simple answer except unlimited free periods! – the difficulty of course is that one can never know when the problems will come. If free periods were spread evenly through the week this would certainly help, and if one had one 'free' each morning and afternoon the situation would be easier.

Other Pastoral Care Heads are unable or unwilling to give the highest priority to their teaching commitments with the consequences noted in a Head of Year's letter describing his pressures and reactions. He also raised two other items of considerable importance in the development of occupational stress:

I often arrive late for my lessons because of the demands of my year work. These include − discipline and pastoral problems that need immediate attention, sick and injured children coming to the year room, parents on the telephone − the list is endless! and all the time knowing that I have a class waiting for me and hoping that they are behaving themselves and, perhaps, most important of all, the worry of knowing that I am responsible for their safety. A great deal of valuable school time is taken up in the 5th year in providing references for employers, etc. I sometimes think employers are getting a very good service for nothing! Often this service is provided at the expense of academic and year work. Another problem is that year work unlike academic work is sometimes difficult to measure in terms of success. This may in turn cause frustration and stress.

These demands, originating from different sources, are important causes of one kind of role conflict for Heads, Deputies, and Heads of Department and pastoral unit teams. But another type can be found in these positions and should not be ignored. This conflict occurs because these management posts contain several parts of other people's roles which are very difficult to integrate into a coherent pattern. These include counsellor, careers adviser, social worker, teacher, manager, resource provider, examiner, secretary, restaurant manager, librarian and adviser (Blackie 1977). A Head of Year identified this kind of role conflict with clarity and humour:

> The main pressure I experience is a result of my dual role as fairy godmother and wicked witch! On the one hand I have to deal firmly and forcefully with a fifteen-year-old bully and yet appear as a sympathetic, approachable, caring person to his classmate in need of help or advice. Members of staff expect us to perform miracles − in the past we have had all classroom discipline problems passed on to us. This is changing gradually and Heads of Department are beginning to take these on, although we keep an overall view of students creating problems in several subject areas. The most difficult miracle to perform is rehabilitation of the social misfit − obviously a difficult task and in some cases impossible. Yet still colleagues refer these students to us with the instructions to 'sort out' so and so . . . he has BO/nobody likes him/he never utters a word to anyone/he sits on a wall on his own all lunchtime, etc. etc. I inevitably attempt to engage this non-communicative individual in a two way conversation(!) and

make what I vainly believe to be helpful suggestions to join the darts club/trampolining club, etc.

The Senior Master of a secondary school identified the different roles he is expected to perform by staff and children. He noted that there was insufficient time in the day to deal effectively with the 'multitude' of daily administrative problems, the counselling of staff and sixth form students and his teaching load. He experienced conflict from the situations in school in which the goodwill of staff, their pooling of ideas and their policy of co-operation were upset by the actions of colleagues who ignored or worked against the staff consensus, or who failed to read and act upon notices or who regarded trivial medical symptoms as sufficient cause to stay away from school. This conflict in the Senior Master's view was analagous to that experienced by the pastoral team leaders who are required to act as personal counsellors and dispensers of disciplinary measures to the same pupils.

Role Expectations of Heads of Primary Schools

A considerable number of role expectations can also be identified in primary schools — at least for Heads. A major factor which has become more apparent recently is the increasing range of demands which are made on them for decisions about matters for which they have had little training or experience. This range includes electrical gadgets — calculators, tape recorders, projectors, computers, typewriters, pottery kilns, duplicating machines, carpentry jobs, boiler house mechanisms, cleaning equipment, playground fixtures and many others. The increasing complexity and sophistication of equipment in schools can be quite a problem — particularly when something breaks down or has to be replaced.

A Head of a primary school recently listed, prior to one of my inservice courses, the jobs which she had been called upon to do during the last few months. It included the following: administrator, supply teacher, supply caretaker, secretary, First Aider, building and safety inspector, technician, social worker, public relations expert, graphics expert, computer programmer, gardener and naturalist. She said that this list was not comprehensive and did not include such things as being the 'listening ear' when the staff come to her with their personal, marital and emotional problems.

Another primary school Head on the same in-service course reported a long list of role demands which she was expected to accept as legitimate parts of her position. She noted her problems under the headings of:

Head Teacher's problems and areas of stress:
(1) The Head Teacher often takes the role of *social worker* and problems range from the potential suicide to looking after children (long after school hours) until the social services can provide overnight accommodation. As the only easily accessible 'professional' much of the Head's time is spent listening to parents' problems connected with loneliness, marital breakdown or neighbour warfare.
(2) *Curriculum development* and the attempt to change attitudes among staff and children can be difficult, and putting new methods and ideas across to parents is a real problem.
(3) Ordinary run-of-the-mill *disaster days* are those when the weather is poor, children are confined indoors, staff tempers short, a queue of parents and a telephone ringing incessantly and the Head Teacher has to take on the role of administrator, social worker, mother, nurse, secretary and teacher in turn. These days tend to get the adrenalin going but leave the Head Teacher exhausted.
(4) *Administration* is a constant bugbear and tends to go to the bottom end of the priority list. Newsletters, forms in triplicate, school fund accounts, and letters to and from the LEA make heavy demands on the Head Teacher.
(5) Perhaps the most frustrating area for me is the time spent on *fund-raising activities*, much of it in my own leisure time, and the need to sort out petty squabbles between parents who don't want to serve on the same stall at the fête, or complain because their children do not win prizes at the fancy dress parade. Having to be polite, friendly and full of gratitude to all-comers is absolutely exhausting.

Role Ambiguity

These areas of conflict for Heads and members of senior and middle management teams do not provide a complete description of the pressures arising from their roles. They have also reported role ambiguity as a major source of stress. This problem arises as a consequence of factors such as: lack of clarity about the scope and responsibilities of their job; uncertainty about what their colleagues expect of them; lack of information required to perform their tasks adequately; uncertainty about how their work is assessed; and doubt about their own career opportunities.

These doubts and uncertainties about roles increase during periods of personal and organisational change. These may occur because of promotion and developments within a school following a new appointment. A Head who had been promoted from a Deputy's post wrote of his feelings of role uncertainty shortly after taking up his new post:

> Without doubt the most stressful period was that between accepting the appointment and the first day of the first term. Although I visited the school on a number of occasions and talked at length with the existing Headmaster and his deputies who were all most helpful, I had no sense of belonging to the organisation. During the holiday period I visited the school regularly, but schools without pupils are strange animals and I felt a strong sense of isolation. Once the term began, the only stress I noticed was that experienced before I addressed the first staff meeting on the first day. Again I had the sensation of being a stranger entering a family gathering. After two weeks this feeling has largely disappeared and I am beginning to feel part of the organisation rather than a decoration on top of the cake. The latter impression was caused because I was uncertain of my role. As a Deputy, or in fact in any other post, I had known what was expected of me. As a new Headmaster there was a distinct diminution of tasks to be accomplished.

For other Heads, unfortunately, there is not the same reduction of ambiguity after promotion. Some of the possible effects of this problem can be identified in the report of the Head of a secondary school who had just completed the first 15 months of her Headship:

> A minority of staff have attempted to sabotage the system by outright antagonism to certain newly-appointed staff and by becoming thoroughly unreasonable towards the pupils, both *en masse* and individually. The children are more reasonable, tolerant, loyal and forgiving than some staff. Some teachers are confused by consultaton and long for a return to dictatorship and the 'close the doors and keep the nasty world out' syndrome. Stress comes from trying to maintain happy working relationships not so much between the staff and me but between warring factions of staff. Stress also comes from a heavy teaching load, as we are 1.3 understaffed, and the urge to teach well, comes from the frustration of heading an expanding

school in a contracting financial situation. The previous Head didn't ask for things when money was available — now I'm asking I get sympathy and a reluctant 'no'. The workload is immense in a situation where a number of people are learning a new role, and I'm chief trainer.

Historically, the Head here makes all decisions and getting people to accept my delegated authority is exhausting. I am unable to stop working, at school and home, therefore I have a very barren social life which is destructive to me. I think this is a fear of not covering all eventualities. Even the most difficult staff have been moved to comment on my voracity for work and how tired I sometimes seem, but I cannot seem to stop. It's a drive to prove that I am doing what they expected: I get depressed when I blame myself for a failure and at the end of a long bad day. I've never contemplated not going to school, but its sometimes with apprehension. Only very occasionally have I thought that if I had enough petrol in the car I would drive to Clifton and jump off the Suspension Bridge.

There are also frequent comments by teachers which suggest that the increasing pace of organisational and curricular changes in schools has resulted in major problems of role ambiguity and role conflict for staff. In order to investigate these pressures I have adapted for use in education, a number of statements which were originally developed for industrial research (Kahn 1973). Teachers were asked to indicate the relevance of each item to their present work experience. There are ten statements which are given below:

Check list of pressures — please tick any which you have experienced this school year.

1. Felt that you had too little authority to carry out your responsibilities.
2. Felt unclear what the scope and responsibilities of your job were.
3. Felt that you had too heavy a workload.
4. Thought that you were not able to satisfy the conflicting demands of your colleagues, parents of pupils, pupils, etc.
5. Did not know how your Head/Head of Department/Pastoral Team Leader evaluated your teaching and tutorial work.
6. Found yourself unable to get the information needed to carry out your job.
7. Felt unable to influence the Head's decisions.

8. Did not know what the people you worked with expected of you.
9. Thought that the amount of work you had to do interfered with how well it was done.
10. Felt that you had to do things at school that were against your better judgement.

I have used this check list frequently in my work with teachers (Dunham 1980a) and information from these small surveys is given in Table 3.1. The first column gives data from an area conference on stress of a LEA when I was one of the contributors. The teachers completed the questionnaire at 9.15 a.m. when the conference started and I reported the results back to them in my discussion of staff stress after lunch. The other results refer to single school staff conferences when I was the tutor for the in-service training day.

The numbers involved in these recent studies are not large but the pattern set by these percentages is sufficiently consistent to add weight to the indications, given in this chapter, that role ambiguity and role conflict are increasing in schools and are now presenting considerable problems to staff. The next chapter is concerned with another major stress situation identified by teachers — the pressures of children's disruptive behaviour and negative attitudes.

Table 3.1: Role Ambiguity and Role Conflict

	Area Conference. All types of schools, 300 teachers, 1977 %	Secondary School A, 43 teachers, 1982 %	Secondary School B, 28 teachers, 1983 %	Secondary School C, 58 teachers, 1983 %
1	13	20	24	22
2	12	37	21	29
3	18	46	78	68
4	15	38	57	50
5	20	32	32	24
6	8	23	10	18
7	18	23	32	49
8	5	20	10	13
9	30	69	82	82
10	23	60	42	29

4 THE PRESSURES OF CHILDREN'S BEHAVIOUR AND ATTITUDES

This chapter is concerned with a number of stress situations which teachers have identified in their work with children who are disruptive; it also considers children's negative attitudes to school, work and staff which are increasingly being reported by teachers as heavy pressures.

The term 'disruptive' is given to a wide range of behaviour problems which includes the pupil who refuses to co-operate and does little or no work in class, and the child who is openly aggressive towards other children and teachers. This range can be seen in a survey conducted amongst the teachers in Clwyd, Wales (1976) in which disruptive behaviour was analysed into six categories which were listed in order of frequency of occurrence as: rowdyism, actual violence, damage to property, threats of violence, theft and sexual misbehaviour. Rowdyism was defined as 'deliberate lateness to lessons, disturbance in the lessons, verbal abuse and refusal to co-operate'.

A survey of what teachers describe as disruptive behaviour has been conducted more recently in two London secondary schools (Lawrence *et al.* 1983). When these teachers talked about acts of disruption they meant rowdiness, abuse, bad language, talking and refusing to accept the teacher's authority. In these schools disruptive behaviour did not take the form of violence or aggression against teachers. This extreme type of disruption is reported in other investigations and these reports suggest that the demands which these kinds of disruptive behaviour make on teachers range from minor infractions to incidents that stretch their coping methods to their limits — and sometimes beyond them.

An insight into these very demanding pressures may be obtained from some of the incidents which have been reported to me: they indicate severe problems in all types of schools. The following two reports are concerned with the behaviour of infant school children. The details were given to me by their teachers for a staff conference which I organised for an in-service training day. The first problem was described by the teacher as an extremely disruptive boy who joined the class in mid-term and caused total disruption. He tore pictures from the wall, threw children's games across the room, scribbled over their work and painting and could not sit beside children without doing something to them. He pinched their faces, pulled their hair, kicked or punched them

33

and put his hand up girls' skirts. If he felt in the least bit rejected or ignored he would inflict injury on himself. Usually this would be biting and scratching his hand until he drew blood. He would scream with pain but refuse to take his hand out of his mouth. The children in the class were petrified of him to begin with and used to keep as far away from him as possible. The teacher said that she had to keep an eye on him every second of the day and was under extreme stress for the whole of the time he was in her class.

In the same school one of her colleagues was attempting to cope with another disruptive boy. She gave me some details of his behaviour:

> His aggressive sessions were usually triggered off by a small and apparently trivial incident. He began by hitting one of the other children and when I intervened his behaviour became increasingly violent. He kicked anything in range. He threw furniture around the room and knocked over anything which stood in his way. He screamed abuse at the top of his voice. My first concern when a mood took him was to get myself between him and the other children. Sometimes I dragged him into the classroom and let him give vent to his pent-up feelings by kicking and punching the walls, the floor and the doors. Sometimes I tried to hold him, having first removed his shoes, which was no easy task. When I reached the end of my tether I sent one of the children for the headmistress who tried to take him back to her room. The main areas of stress were the uncertainty of not knowing when he would react like that, the bites, cuts and bruises.

The next report is concerned with a child in a primary school which was sent to me by the Headteacher. The child was eleven years old and had been in the school 2½ years. Johnny was known by the staff as a 'loner' and as a boy who was not popular with his peers. The incident which the Head described had happened a week before my in-service training day for the primary school Heads in an LEA. It concerned one of the dinner supervisors who told this boy and another boy to stop fighting. Johnny then ran off. The dinner supervisor asked for the assistance of a teacher because she thought that Johnny had run away from school. The teacher found the boy by one of the school gates in a very sullen mood and he seemed quite unprepared to chat with the teacher or co-operate in any way. The teacher asked Johnny to go inside the building but Johnny lost his temper and threw a tantrum. He clung to the railings in an act of defiance at co-operation. When the teacher managed eventually to get the child into the building and sat him down, he was still in a most unco-operative frame of mind. The dinner supervisor had told the teacher that Johnny had been abusive to her when she had asked him to stop bullying a younger child. But according to Johnny the dinner supervisor had not understood that they were fighting in a friendly way rather than in a temper.

During the interview with the teacher, Johnny was gasping and catching his breath the whole time in the most affected way. He was taken to his classroom and asked to sit down at his desk. He did so and appeared to be calmer. A little while later the teacher checked that he was still in his classroom and found at that time that Johnny was crunching something in his mouth. As he told the teacher that he had eaten his dinner, he was then asked what he was eating. He showed the remains of a pencil and the teacher to quote his own words 'was staggered to see his mouth was crammed full of pencil and that he was apparently eating it'.

In the secondary school some of the severest forms of disruptive behaviour which teachers have to contend with can be illustrated by the report to me by the Head of House in a comprehensive school of two boys aged 14 and 15 respectively. The fourteen-year-old's behaviour was described by the Head of House as extremely disruptive and he gave details of what he meant by this description:

He came to us at the beginning of the second year. He was placed in a remedial form but even here he is well behind the other children. Progress is very slow and he retains little but he has occasional flashes of insight. He is extremely disruptive and often downright dangerous in practical lessons. He *will* not sit still and in fact jogs and dances round the room. Even when seated, he continually mutters and talks to himself and others and he is often obscene and aggressive to staff. He is a bully (a big boy for his age), sometimes just for the sake of it e.g. making other boys eat cigarettes — or worse; but more often in order to extort money (or anything else he takes a fancy to) from other children. However it is very difficult to prove this as most children are too frightened to complain.

For the sake of the other children and after much deliberation we requested that he be removed from the school. However the parents absolutely refused even though they have no control over the boy. Being part of the school is obviously benefiting the boy himself. He loves school, was very proud to take part in sports day and to play rugby for the school. Unfortunately, it is the other children who are suffering while he gains, socially, academically and financially.

The fifteen-year-old boy had created many problems at school such as petty theft and the more serious stealing of dangerous chemicals from the school laboratories. He disrupted lessons by refusing to work. He wrote obscene letters to the staff and gave details which meant they could be easily traced to him. He suspended smaller pupils from second-storey windows by their hands. He broke into school at the week-end and vandalised the main offices. During his illegal time in school he let off the fire extinguishers.

The Head of House in his report to me tried to analyse why the behaviour of these two boys caused him so much stress:

> In my position as Head of House I have to try and balance the pupil's interest against the staff and the philosophy of the school. This has led to confrontation with junior staff, senior staff and finally the Head. In many instances the staff found the pupil's antics to be highly amusing e.g. pretending to be a dead fly during art lessons. However when indiscipline crept in then staff gave up and wanted me to deal with it. Parental support for the boy was negligible. The final conflict was a head-on clash with the Head over the pupil's suspension resulting in disciplinary action against myself being threatened. The pupil was suspended on many occasions and put into a unit for disruptive pupils. I felt that I was always fighting a losing battle against the staff who were not interested in the long-term problem.

The role conflict of Heads of House and Year who are the people-in-the-middle of the opposing forces of staff, Headteacher and pupils presents major problems because the feelings aroused by teaching disruptive children can be very strong.

These children are often very angry and so their teachers often encounter, what one of them described as 'raw emotion', from a number of pupils in and out of class.

This strong emotion may be expressed in different ways: aggressiveness or attention-seeking behaviour or a lack of consideration for other people or unfriendly attitudes towards them. For teachers who do not think that teaching is concerned with the raw emotions of anger the expression of it in a classroom or school can be a distressing experience. For teachers whose personal values and experience have led them to believe that the right way to deal with angry feelings is to 'swallow' or hide them, it can be a frightening experience to be faced with children and young adults who do not seem to share their inhibitions. These teachers are sometimes out of their depth emotionally and, therefore, another major source of stress in teaching disruptive children is insecurity which is increased by the unpredictability of the pupils' behaviour. This perspective was clearly formulated by a perceptive teacher in a school for maladjusted children who wrote:

> Insecurity is the cause of much stress amongst the people I work with, and it appears to be the result of the unpredictability of the behaviour of the children. The staff rarely know what to expect next and this threatens their security by reducing their control over their environment. This insecurity is increased by direct confrontations with children, especially when they are hostile as a group towards us, either individually or collectively and they do naturally exploit this. Another source of insecurity is lack of psychological knowledge, a feeling that one is out of one's depth with a particular child, or the school as a whole. This is particularly pertinent when an adult is faced with a hostile reaction which is not understood; the adult then tends either to feel intellectually inadequate, or worse still, can take the hostile reaction personally.

A further source of insecurity for teachers is that the range of the pupils' behaviour and attitudes is beyond the teachers' experience, training and expectations. In these circumstances staff working with me say that they feel confused and uncertain about the right actions to take. These pressures can be identified in the following two comments. The first was given by a tutor in a secondary school:

> There is no racial tension between the boys in my tutor group – they are well integrated. The same is not true of the girls, who have isolated themselves into groups according to colour/religion. I am *very* concerned about this situation and at a complete loss as to the best action, if any, to take.

The second report contains a question which I am often asked. The problem was described by a Head of Year:

> He is a first-year boy who is an overweight and unattractive child. He continually pesters staff at every opportunity and demands

attention with repetitive questions. He is inclined to daydream in class but pretends to work hard. Older children plague him and every playtime he seeks refuge by following the staff on duty. He seldom plays with his peers but when he does he causes embarrassment by touching and kissing them and by making occasional declarations of love. He is the youngest child of overbearing parents. What can we do to help him now before our patience has worn too thin?

I was invited into this Head of House's school to discuss with the tutors of the fifth year pupils some of the problems caused by their behaviour and attitudes. They presented me with the following list which the tutors said contained the names of the children they did not understand and wanted help with.

1. Barry

He spent much of the beginning of the fifth year away from school and he is generally disaffected. His tutor has tried to get him into school because he was in trouble in his fourth year for truancy and there is a strong possibility that he will be taken to court and his family fined. When we asked the EWO to visit the family we found that his mother now had a new boy friend and that Barry did not like him. After this visit Barry came to school and he said that he was not coming to school because his mum and the new man want to get engaged and he does not want to live with them. He believes that if he stays away from school he will eventually be taken to court and put into care, which is what he wants. Where do we do from here?

2. Peter

Peter's problem is stealing keys. It doesn't seem to be just a passing adolescent phase as he has had treatment for disturbed behaviour earlier and there have been stealing incidents before. Unfortunately, his influence has spread, even though he tends to be a loner, to a new boy, Mick, who has also become involved in minor stealing incidents. Do we make sure that there is never ever any opportunity for him to steal or do we try to give him the opportunity to develop responsibility and honesty and actually give him keys to look after and fetch?

3. Brian

He is the youngest of four children. He has a record of truancy, lying, theft, idleness and disruptive behaviour. He is definitely underperforming though it is thought by the staff that he is certainly not as clever as his father believes. Father is repressive and unsympathetic with his son and argues with the mother in front of the boy: he blames the school for not making the boy work harder. If Brian does any homework his father demands to see it and on one occasion tore it up after telling his son that it was rubbish. The boy now only works when forced to by staff. The subject teachers find it difficult to give him the attention he needs. They are often thankful if he is quiet. What do you suggest?

4. Joyce

She first became awkward towards the end of the first year when she started avoiding PE. Throughout the second year she refused to take part in this subject. During the third year she was frequently in trouble for lateness and smoking and often ran home after a confrontation. On one of these occasions she bit the senior mistress. She has now become a serious problem seldom managing to complete a full day in school, and she was shoplifting during these absences. Throughout her school 'carecr' the parents were consulted regularly but with no real co-operation. Mother refused to accept that there was a problem even though she had no control over the child herself. She had also been seeing the Educational Psychologist who eventually decided she was maladjusted and should not be in our school. However, in practice this made little difference as there were no places available in schools for maladjusted children. Joyce says that she hates this school. The Head of another school was persuaded to accept her on the condition that she put in a full week's attendance with us. That was June 1978 — so far she has not put in a full day!! Where did we go wrong?

5. Neil

Neil belongs to an upper middle-class family. He is underachieving and will gain fewer exam successes than he should. He is often abstracted in class. On the cover of one of his exercise books he wrote recently:

> I don't know and I don't fucking care. I'm going to kill me mum and dad, and tear out all my hair. KILL KILL KILL.

Do we take this seriously?

This wide range of problems is very demanding but the number of less extreme kinds of behaviour is also a considerable source of stress. The Head of an Avon comprehensive school was thinking about this type of heavy load when he wrote:

> The teachers' energy is drained by the necessity of being always on the alert to contain outbreaks of antisocial behaviour, to meet insolence without losing self-control and to cool the tempers of those whose frustration drives them into conflict with their peers (Simpson 1974).

A Head of House in the same school argued on one of my courses that for staff in positions of responsibility, particularly in pastoral work, stress was inevitable because teachers had to become involved in the pupils' problems. To avoid stress it was necessary to remain uninvolved and 'to walk past the non-uniformed pupil, the disruption, the fights, the litter and all those day-to-day events which create stress'. But if the teacher did this, he argued, the member of staff would be useless in the job.

When involvement in the pupils' behaviour is matched by involvement in the pupils' problems, staff experience further stress because they feel that they can do little to help the pupils to cope with the pressures which make them disruptive. Staff report that they feel helpless and hopeless because they are powerless to change the conditions in which the children live. Some of these circumstances were identified in a research project carried out by a Deputy Head in Northampton (Bispham 1980). He interviewed pupils in secondary schools who had been reported by their teachers to be behaviour problems, and a few brief statements from his interviews provide an outline of the daily heavy pressures they experience:

> I look out of our front door at the street and wonder if I'll ever manage to get away from it all. There must be a different sort of life somewhere.

> Mum teaches us all to 'nick'. I know it's terrible but it's true. I've never been caught but I feel it's not right.

> My home is all untidy and nobody knows whats going on. That's why I like school to be orderly and well organised.

> I want to get on with people but I lack practice. My four brothers tease me and girls are bitchy about my deaf sister, so how can I learn?

Homework is all right for a lot of kids, especially when you've got small families and their parents understand. But, tell me, how do you think I get it done in a place like ours? The kids tear the books, and get jam on everything. Telly never stops. 'Use your bedroom', says the teacher. Is he kidding, it's even worse there and I share it with two others. Homework isn't very realistic for a lot of us. Is it really necessary?

The feelings of impotence which teachers may develop as they learn about these circumstances were clearly formulated by a Headteacher in a primary school, in response to my request for information about the stress situations she experienced in school:

I seem to fight a losing battle as many home standards conflict with mine. Some days I despair of the future when I see pupils' home circumstances. Some of the children just haven't a chance. That's when I get a feeling of deep frustration and wonder if anything I have tried to do will have any long-term effect.

A teacher in a secondary school built in a big council estate had resigned because she could no longer cope with the work pressures she identified for me before my staff conference in her school. She wrote:

The causes of stress for me are the poor discipline in pupils, particularly the coarse language; unsolicited rudeness and constant talking; teaching very low ability classes at the end of the day; losing free periods which are needed for preparation, duplicating, etc; having to cover for a colleague who is not pulling her weight; noise and the constant battle to create a stimulating but tranquil and ordered environment in the classroom. I feel I'm a zoo-keeper, not a teacher. I have never before been so aware of differences between teachers and pupils. My initial reaction is to laugh it off and turn the whole thing into a joke. This leads to some very cruel 'fun' in the staffroom − I hear myself expressing attitudes which basically are against my principles e.g. 'Ann should have been drowned at birth.' Deep down one feels a sense of outrage and anger that schools like this should exist, that the system is being perpetuated because there are very few pupils who can set a reasonable standard of behaviour or who have a real interest in education. Underlying all this is a terrible sense of sadness at having to witness wasted lives and opportunities.

The feelings of not being able to make an adequate contribution to the solution of the pupils' problems are compounded by communication difficulties between teachers and other professional workers. The children who are disruptive in school have often also come to the attention of the police, probation officers, child guidance clinics, health and social services and, therefore, the disruptive pupil is often a multi-disciplinary problem rather than simply an educational one. But inter-professional contact and communication is sometimes reported (Dunham 1981b) to be ineffective and frustrating rather than supportive. One teacher in a secondary school put the matter bluntly:

> There are too many people who offer hypothetical advice. When we seek support beyond the bounds of the school, too often the problem is referred back to us as though we had done nothing to deal with the problem.

When there are significant barriers to the flow of information between the services concerned with the needs of children, teachers complain about a lack of information from other professional workers. Child guidance services and social workers seem to get most of the blame. Some of the difficulties were identified by the Headmaster of a special school in his report to me:

> The importance of the issue of confidentiality is causing inter-professional difficulties. The information we want we may not get. Closer communication is needed with the Child Guidance Clinics and the medical services. If you do not have a medical degree you will not get any information. The rapid staff turn-over in Social Services also causes great problems – for instance – one of my children has had six changes in the supervising social worker in the last two years.

These difficulties in interprofessional communication can also be seen in the report by a psychiatrist (Skynner 1975) of an attempt to improve communication between his Child Guidance teams and the teachers in a secondary school who were involved in the care of disruptive children. The clinic team – psychiatrist, psychologist, psychiatric social worker and child psychotherapist – visited the school every month for two years to discuss with the staff the pupils who were problems in the school. The psychiatrist described the contact and interaction between the teachers and the clinic team as the experiment progressed. At the first meeting there was a large attendance, perhaps about 30 teachers in all. There may have been a feeling among the teachers that the large group situation was too chaotic because the senior staff altered the arrangements for our second visit without prior agreement or warning. Only four teachers were present and it was explained to us that they were the only ones concerned in the case. The third visit brought a crisis for the team. They arrived on time to find the library, where they held their meetings, locked. The teachers were still eating and they paid little attention to the presence of the team. But gradually the teachers' confidence to offer contributions increased and their capacity to tolerate open disagreement grew. But these developments were not continuous: a marked advance would often be followed by a partial regression, a well attended and lively session followed by lateness, absence and seemingly unrewarded interchange. In one session the team found themselves once again locked out; the teachers were eating; almost everyone was late, with no excuses made; and the discussion of cases seemed inconclusive and marked by indifference and fragmentation, people often talking together in two's or three's . . . But the psychiatrist reported that at the end of two years there appeared to have been a reduction in inter-group conflict and stereotyping and the development of good professional relationships. He supported these conclusions by noting that staff spoke of the ability they now had to share problems and communicate about them, as well as the confidence they now possessed that they could cope.

If the attempts of the clinic team had facilitated a greater degree of sharing amongst staff teaching disruptive children they would have reversed a trend towards isolation which some observers have claimed is characteristic of the way teachers work. A team of research workers (Galloway *et al.* 1982), who investigated the effects of special classes for disruptive pupils in Sheffield, wrote:

Teaching can be an extraordinarily lonely profession. The loneliness of the classroom is compounded by that of the staffroom. Disruptive behaviour is the most striking example of stress which too often has to be borne in painful isolation. For many teachers, admitting to bad classroom discipline is paramount to admitting that they are bad teachers.

There may also be an absence of support for those teachers with responsibilities for teaching disruptive pupils because their colleagues may feel reluctant to offer assistance because to do so would imply their incompetence. Many who join my in-service courses appear not to have experienced much support in their schools. They seem to have had few opportunities to discuss their stress situations. They seem surprised to find acceptance and not cynicism as they are encouraged to express their feelings and release their emotional blocks. A Head of Department in a comprehensive school told me of her expectations before she came to one of my courses and her growing awareness of an alternative approach to teachers who want to talk about their problems:

> As a result of previous experience I came with a guarded attitude and I feel I was aggressive towards you at times, something for which I apologise. In fact I thought you were most caring in the way you posed your penetrating questions and comments. I was glad to be made aware without being made to feel inadequate, criticised or condemned as has been my previous experience in school. I certainly feel more able to cope and more willing to lend a sympathetic ear to those who feel at the end of their tether.

The difficulties which staff experience with their colleagues in relation to the teaching of disruptive children have another dimension. It may be thought by some staff that to a significant extent school policy and teacher behaviour are responsible for disruptive behaviour. The research of the Deputy Head in Northampton, which was discussed earlier in this chapter, provides some information in support of this argument. A few brief statements from his interviews will indicate what I mean:

> There's eight of us stick together all the time. We cause a lot of trouble but they still leave us together. Maybe they don't care anyway.

> This school pretends. It doesn't really care about anybody. It's just a face it puts on.

> I enjoyed the first two years at secondary school but the rest was dreadful.

> I suppose I was disappointed with the third, fourth and fifth years. It was all the same thing with the same equipment but not enough of it. In fact, it was the same old making do.

Men accept me as a woman. I know men fancy me and I enjoy it. But here I'm just another silly little kid.

Sometimes a teacher calls me 'shorty' or 'fatso'. It isn't fair. I hate it and I try to pay them back.

Support for the point of view that a school's organisation and relationships are important factors in the development of disruptive behaviour can also be found in the report of the study of special classes for disruptive children in ten Sheffield secondary schools (Galloway *et al.* 1982). The research team found large differences between these schools in the number of incidents reported by staff which caused them 'genuine concern or stress extending beyond their day-to-day problems'. At one school 33 per cent of the teachers interviewed could not think of an incident which had caused them real concern in the current school year (most of the interviews took place in the spring term). In contrast over 85 per cent of teachers at two other schools could think of disruptive incidents which has caused them real concern in the present term. Frequently the incident was within the previous two weeks. The teachers in the ten schools were asked about sources of support in dealing with disruptive behaviour. In six schools the formal channels for dealing with problem pupils involved referral upwards – teachers were expected to refer to the Head of Department or to the Year Tutor, who if necessary would 'hand-on' the pupil to the Deputy Head, who in turn would pass the problem to the Head. Staff tension and frustration developed because these channels were found to be unsatisfactory: they were too slow; they did not give enough support to teachers at the rough end of the pupils' behaviour; and it was felt that senior staff did not appreciate their difficulties. In these schools it was implied that asking for help was a sign of weakness.

In the schools with the smallest number of reported incidents it was a firm aspect of school policy that the form tutor was much more than the first point of referral: this was the point of the first action. It was, therefore, necessary for the tutor to know not only the pupils in the tutor group but also their parents. It was also strongly emphasised that effective school policy for coping with problem behaviour depended on consultation between staff. The Sheffield team give an illustration of these two approaches in their report of a form tutor whose problem was that a girl with an Italian mother was being called a 'Wop bitch' and other offensive names. The tutor told the Senior Mistress about her concern. She was advised to deal with the matter in her tutor group.

She talked to the girls involved and the problem was resolved without escalating it upwards to a higher management level. The tutor received support and encouragement in dealing with the problem herself and so her confidence was strengthened.

This report is a clear indication of the strength of staff support in coping with the pressures of children's antisocial behaviour and attitudes. It is, therefore, important to be aware that stress may reduce teachers' involvement in pastoral care and their willingness to provide supportive relationships in school. The interaction between disruptive pupil behaviour and stress in teaching is a two-way process: the former can be either a cause or an effect of the latter. This interaction will be explored more fully in the chapter concerned with stress reactions (Chapter Eight) but meanwhile, in the next chapter, I want to discuss the exacerbating effects of poor working conditions.

5 THE PRESSURES OF DIFFICULT WORKING CONDITIONS

When the environment in which teachers work is poor three important kinds of pressures are generated: physical, financial and organisational. The physical aspects of poor working conditions include badly constructed buildings with inadequate soundproofing and high noise levels and split-site schools with the consequent difficulties of commuting between buildings. The financial aspects are becoming increasingly significant. Reduced school budgets have meant lower levels of expenditure on equipment and textbooks and smaller LEA funds have resulted in the redeployment of teachers, redundancies, school closures, narrowing of promotion opportunities and the restriction of career prospects. The organisational aspects include difficult and frustrating staff relationships which may result in little support of junior staff by top management, poor co-operation between the academic and pastoral concerns and conflict between departments and teams and between cliques in the staffroom. The major consequences of poor communications include conflict about different aspects of school policy and time pressures because of poor planning of issues such as meetings and deadlines. These organisational pressures are often related to the management styles of the Head and Deputies.

Several of these environmental pressures can be identified in the following list, which I compiled for a staff development conference, of poor working conditions in one secondary school:

(a) Lack of sanctions to deal with persistent 'rule breakers' who virtually ignore staff. This is particularly difficult when on duty outside the classroom.

(b) General noise, disorderly behaviour, ill manners, foul language, litter, etc. in and around the school at 'break' and lunch times.

(c) The lack of facilities provided for some subjects — particularly practical ones — and their gradual run-down because of wearing out, non-replacement of equipment and vandalism.

(d) The provision of inadequate funds to provide material and books necessary for teaching a subject in an interesting way. The annual amount provided has in some cases not increased over the past five to six years.

(e) Class sizes too large for practical subjects — particularly outdoors — with potentially dangerous equipment.

(f) Teaching mixed ability groups with a variation between 'O level' ability and virtual illiteracy. Also teaching groups where some pupils are taking an examination and others in the group are not and the latter are therefore not motivated and may be in and out of the class because of work experience or absenteeism.

(g) The conditions under which we are expected to work, e.g. no proper office or desk, and little secretarial assistance.

(h) Little or no ancillary help for practical work, hence all experiments have to be set up, glassware washed and equipment maintained by the teacher in the non-teaching periods which should be used for lesson preparation and pastoral work.

(i) Having to be at the receiving end of ill-tempered 'superiors'.

Physical Aspects of Poor Working Conditions

Further aspects of the three types of environmental pressures can also be identified in teachers' reports. The physical aspects include old schools which often present considerable structural difficulties. A report from a teacher in a primary school illustrates this problem and shows the importance of limitations of space:

> The biggest source of pressure in this school, built in 1888, is the physical lack of space, within and without the building. The classrooms have high windows, the playground space is limited and there is no grassy area. The hall which is in use all day, also serves as a dining area involving the shortage of tables and chairs as well as PE climbing equipment. We have new exciting equipment which requires storage in an easily accessible place. Finding a place proves extremely difficult and entails constant re-thinking. The display of children's work uses space which is at a premium and which needs to be carefully thought out to avoid damage. The lack of space is, of course, accentuated by high class numbers. The dinner hour causes pressure as most of the children stay either for lunch or sandwiches and there is pressure throughout the morning and afternoon breaks with so many children to supervise. The large numbers prove also very difficult for untrained Welfare ladies to manage which gives rise to tension.

New schools also confront teachers with inadequate working conditions. The need to save money on building costs has resulted in the
erection of poorly constructed buildings with inadequate sound insula-
tion between classrooms. Some teachers express anger at being disturbed and some are resentful of the criticisms they receive from their
colleagues about the talking, shouting and movement they allow in
their classes while others react to high levels of noise apathetically.
Newly built primary schools have tended to incorporate open-plan
designs. Here, too, higher noise levels have been reported and their
possible significance in the development of stress has been identified by
the Headteacher of a first school who reported that her two most
stressful years in teaching were those spent as Deputy Head of a new
open-plan infant school. Stress was caused by a number of factors: she
did not agree with the Head's organisation of the school but because of
her sense of loyalty she did not criticise her in the staffroom; she was
experimenting with a new method of teaching reading which gave dis-
appointing results; the open-plan design forced her to change her
accustomed teaching patterns as she had to work closely with another
member of staff which brought complications but little benefit. Her
summary of these two years was:

I became accustomed to the complications but I always found the
noise excessively tiring.

There are research reports of further consequences for people who
work in prolonged noisy environments, though little attention has been
given to their possible harmful effects in schools. Research in industry
(Eysenck 1975) has established that noise can damage hearing and can
have psychological effects of poor concentration and sudden changes
of mood. The damage to hearing is related to the gradual development
of chronic deafness and a person is at risk of this disability after exposure to noise levels exceeding 90 decibels. Research has indicated
the noise levels in decibels of different noise sources, which are given
in Table 5.1.

It would be helpful to compare these decibel counts with the results
of monitoring school noises but I have little information to offer. In
one inner-city secondary school where I participated as the consultant
in a staff development conference, daily records were kept for a week
by the local Environment Health Officer and showed decibel counts of
65–75.

In a new comprehensive school the noise level of one particular

Table 5.1: Decibel Levels of Some Sources of Noise

Noise Source	Noise Levels in Decibels
Circular saw	75–105
Motor-cycles	81–98
Very busy city street	90
Foundry	95–115

Source: Eysenck (1975).

source was monitored and reported to me by a Head of Department:

> We have a system of bells which serve to signal the end of lessons and fire alarms. Recently an over-zealous Fire Officer decreed that bells, which had been adequate for the dual purpose for twenty years, must be replaced with gongs designed for external fire alarms. These have been installed on landings, where children are constantly interviewed by staff and in our newest building, over the teacher's blackboard. One of these measures 102 decibels at six feet. It is a source of actual pain and dread.

These reports suggest the importance of considering noise as a contributory factor in the development of stress. But there is one more stress situation which should be identified before this discussion of the physical aspects of poor working conditions is concluded. This is concerned with the erection of widely spaced buildings in new schools and the use of existing buildings on different sites as split-site schools. Teachers here have to contend with what is described as a 'brisk five minute walk between lessons carrying books and equipment' or a 'sharp ten minute drive in the car to the main building'. An example of the difficulties which can be caused by split-site working was presented by the Deputy Head of a secondary school:

> The staff managed fairly well if they could be away from the main school all morning or all afternoon, but this was not always possible and much time was spent travelling to and fro, carrying books etc. which was tiring especially if wet. Pastoral care/communications between staff or staff and girls were not always adequate, staff absence and cover were much more difficult to arrange especially when it concerned staff without cars, as the day-to-day contact with each other was severely diminished.

On-site problems are also encountered as a teacher in a new comprehensive school reported:

> My major pressures are having to move a good deal between lessons in a crowded school; coping with great numbers of pupils outside the classroom as well as in it and finding that the teaching spaces used for other purposes are often left in an unfit or vandalised state which has a very demoralising effect.

Financial Pressures

The second kind of environmental pressure which teachers are having to cope with is financial. The effects can be recognised in the deterioration of some of the physical aspects of the school but most directly they have been felt in the classroom. The lack of money for school resources has hampered the development of new courses and has blocked the use of updated textbooks. But the contraction of the Education Service has placed more general burdens on staff. The Head of a primary school described one of these more general problems:

> A year ago we had 9 staff for 200 children; now we have 4½ staff for 136 children. The 4½ staff are trying to continue all the activities we had before staff were redeployed.

These worries are felt most keenly by Heads and they will be discussed more fully in the next chapter. But many staff are affected by radical changes in career expectations, particularly those teachers who entered the profession with a vertical model of achievement based on promotion. In the early part of their careers this model matched reality: they were, for example, promoted to middle management positions in their late twenties or early thirties with the strong assumption that further progress would follow. These assumptions are now at risk and a painful analysis of their professional and personal development is a common theme in my discussions with them. These risks of non-achievement to the holders of middle management positions and scale 2 and 3 posts are presenting entirely new kinds of problems because their whole previous work experience has been spent in a period of expansion (Bone 1983).

Organisational Pressure

The third kind of environmental pressure caused by difficult working situations is organisational. These problems include ineffective communications, difficult staff relationships, very heavy workloads and inappropriate leadership styles.

Ineffective Communications

Communication problems have frequently been identified by teachers. One is concerned with poor sharing of information between different groups of teachers within a school — between departments and houses and between the academic and pastoral teams. Another problem is caused by inadequate information transmission between the senior management team and staff, leading to uncertainty and confusion. An example of this kind of situation was given by a head of a geography department in a comprehensive school:

> The geography department met to consider the issue of stress and this paper represents the views expressed at the meeting. There were differences of opinion on the extent of stress on staff. However, some areas did provoke comment and could be identified. A principal factor causing stress was thought to be organisational. It was considered that the fragmented nature of much of the daily running of the school produced an environment which was responsible for many mistakes being made by staff. Many of the procedures for members of staff are at best vague and roles are ill-defined, so that new members of staff in particular can make wrong decisions and do not always know who to approach with a problem. This can produce anxiety and even fear of reproach from Senior Staff.

Difficult Staff Relationships

Further details of poor vertical communication between senior management and staff were given by teachers when I interviewed them in preparation for a staff development conference in 1978. Their poor opinion of the organisational climate in which they worked is clearly indicated in the following statements:

(a) There is a constant air of criticism, never of support and praise.
(b) There is the frustration of being unable to speak openly and frankly on matters felt to be adversely affecting the school.
(c) There is an over-emphasis on meetings, discussions, etc. which

all have a negative end because the decisions have already been made.

(d) The directions (from administration) are given late and with little time for implementation.

(e) There is excessive information to absorb from papers.

(f) Inadequate time is given for administrative tasks.

(g) Inconsistent styles of communication cause stress. Some decisions and administrative arrangements are communicated in a courteous manner, in good time and on a person-to-person level, and so stress is caused if others are delivered in a curtly worded document at the eleventh hour.

(h) There is a lack of consultation and communication, particularly the latter, on the part of management leading to the 'cog in the wheel syndrome'.

(i) There are inconsistent instructions in administrative procedures.

These teachers also reported difficult staff relationships as major organisational pressures. These difficulties are identified in the following statements which are quoted from my interviews:

(a) There are new situations requiring new skills and attitudes but some members of staff suffer from an inability or an unwillingness to change.

(b) Staff who are inexperienced, inadequate, poorly trained or simply unprofessional are an obvious burden to their more conpetent colleagues.

(c) Some teachers here occasionally lack sensitivity or have insufficient knowledge of the individual child, thus creating potentially explosive situations arising out of relatively trivial incidents.

(d) Newly qualified members of staff are often ill-equipped in teaching the basic skills. They become cynical or disillusioned when faced with the reality of the teaching situation. Weaknesses, doubts and feelings of guilt about their performance are often repressed.

(e) The occasions when fellow members of staff proved unreliable led to pressure since one was never quite certain whether one would be let down again.

(f) Most 'stress' caused by teachers themselves who are too bloody idle to meet demands head on and constantly carp about children whilst they themselves, mostly long-haired lefties complete with beards and anoraks, couldn't teach a frog to jump. I get more annoyed with staff than I do with kids.

Heavy Workloads

The next source of organisational stress to be discussed occurs more frequently in my reports than either poor communications or difficult staff relationships. This consists of heavy workloads which, in conjunction with inadequate time to complete them, create the characteristic pressure situation of attempting to do more work in less time. When this situation is compounded by teachers concluding that there is a lack of recognition, appreciation and understanding of their increased effort, their feelings of frustration are heightened. These problems were identified clearly and sensitively in a letter from a Deputy Head of a comprehensive school:

> Last week you said that the Head had indicated that I did some staff counselling. I don't actually see myself in that role. I think my office is simply a place to where some staff come when they are upset and I really only listen. However, as I look back over the last year and think about the reasons why staff have come to talk, the main ones would seem to be:
> (i)   a feeling of having too much to do
> (ii) a feeling of not being valued.
> Often these two reasons have been linked together in other words the feeling of not being valued has come at a time when they felt they were (or had just been) working particularly hard, thus the feeling has been expressed that only that which is wrongly done is mentioned, while the good is given little recognition.

There is another aspect of the workload/time factor which needs to be considered. The problem is not only that teachers may not be able to complete all the tasks they are given or set for themselves. It is also, importantly, a question of not being able to achieve a level of performance in important aspects of their work which would bring good, warm feelings of a job well done.

The feelings which are generated when teachers have not been able to do their work as well as they think it should be done are clearly identified in two reports from secondary school teachers:

> I really think that at times I have so much work to do that I do not

stand a chance of completing it well. I feel special anxiety due to a new A level course that I am teaching. I have no detailed knowledge of much of the syllabus, no help and no readily available source material. I feel my responsibility very much to the A level students and live in constant fear that if they fail A level it will be my fault. I must spend more time on their work but with everything else I find that I'm just too tired most evenings to put in the extra work.

The second report suggests how long standing these feelings can be:

The response to these situations is a guilty feeling nearly all the time that nothing has been done properly and when I do try to relax I feel that I should be doing something in the way of preparation. This even applies during the holidays. Since starting teaching I have never been able to feel that everything has been completed satisfactorily and that I am properly prepared. There are many long-term projects on which I would like to spend time, but they are constantly shelved because there are more pressing and immediate demands.

The pressures and feelings which are referred to in these reports are , I think, intensified by the perception that the time and effort which could be given to important tasks is being wasted on matters which are unimportant and probably useless. These are non-teaching activities: interruptions, telephone calls, paper work and meetings which seem fruitless because nothing seems resolved after hours of discussion or because the significant decisions are taken by the Head or Senior Management Team. There are also frequent complaints about the time spent (and wasted) on pastoral and tutorial duties. One teacher gave a clear statement of this point of view:

A great deal of time was spend pursuing pastoral matters which tended to detract from one's teaching. This type of occurrence created a certain type of pressure, i.e. teacher or social worker.

Inappropriate Leadership Styles

The issues of meetings and decision making without consultation discussed in these reports are important aspects of another source of organisational stress caused by poor working conditions. This source is the leadership of Headteachers. The consequences for staff of Heads' styles of leadership are important because of the power in the role to make significant decisions about pupils and teachers. This influence and the different ways it is used are still crucial factors in the attitudes, experience and expectations of staff. The reports which I receive from staff provide continuing support for the argument that: 'The Head-teacher exerts the most pressure and stress on his teachers. His attitudes and conceptions and the teachers' conceptions of his role can determine whether the school is a good place to work and can therefore reduce the amount of stress' (Hoyle 1969).

Unfortunately for some teachers, my reports suggest support for the more negative view that Heads' actions may increase staff stress and may make the school a place of frustration, anxiety, anger, threat and fear. The general comments of a scale 2 PE teacher provide a good introduction to a discussion of this perspective:

> In our present system of education, Heads are all powerful and so most teachers, if they wish to be successful, must please the Head. The Head often does not have the charisma, experience or relevant qualifications to cope with the power which is attributed to him. Heads are usually good teachers, but they have little or no manage-ment training. To be successful they must have a thoughtful ap-proach to their style of management otherwise the problems of poor communications, insecurity and job inefficiency occur in staff. If the Head is weak one has to grin and bear it. One must stay on the right side of him to achieve promotion for which one needs a good refer-ence and for favourable considerations within the school for status and for material benefits such as equipment.

Other characteristics of the Head in addition to weakness are reported to cause difficulties for staff. These include: autocratic leader-ship behaviour which ignores consultation and refuses to delegate decision making and authority; indecisive or ambiguous leadership behaviour which does not provide clear and helpful guidelines for teachers, and unpredictability or inconsistency which generates staff uncertainty and insecurity.

A situation of long-standing uncertainty was described in an inter-view with a teacher in an infants school. The behaviour of the Head was so unpredictable that the staff felt apprehensive about her actions and decisions. Announcements were made by the Headmistress to the whole school not only in morning assembly but at any time that she wished. She praised or criticised children and teachers indiscriminately. The staff attempted to cope with her unpredictable behaviour in different ways. My interviewee used a lot of physical activities such as painting the walls of her large house to release the frustration she developed in school. These personal resources were not sufficient to meet the demands caused by her poor work environment and she felt guilty when she had no patience left in the evening to help her own children with their homework.

Another kind of leadership behaviour which generates staff frustration is indecisiveness or ambiguity. It also causes confusion, conflict and much wasted effort. When a Deputy Head identified her major stress situations in her present school as the ambiguous leadership style of her Head she provided some details which may enable us to understand her problems and perhaps to see similarities with poor management in other schools.

The Deputy Head reported that a new appointment of second Deputy had recently been made and that this had caused a lot of confusion about areas of responsibility at the top management level. The new Deputy had taken over, with the Head's authority, certain projects in the school, which the Senior Mistress would have been responsible for before the appointment. There is conflict between the Deputy and the Senior Mistress about these projects, with supporters among the staff for both sides. The Senior Mistress complains about a lack of information and the Deputy complains that she is being criticised for only doing her duty. The Head declines to make any decisions himself about these problems, which the top management team cannot solve. It is difficult to see how they will be resolved.

This situation of the Head's reluctance to make decisions which causes frustration and worry for staff is not confined to the problem of overlapping boundaries of responsibilities among members of the senior management team. Nor is it restricted to the Head's behaviour. The pressures on staff are also caused by the actions of the senior management team as they interact with Heads of Department, Heads of Year and House and staff. The focus of teachers' requests for decisions from Heads and Deputies is frequently the pupils' behaviour and some of the strongest and loudest demands are concerned with disruptive children. When the senior staff are indecisive in these circumstances, when they say they need to consult with social workers or probation officers before coming to a decision, the junior staff concerned feel a lack of support at a critical time which they resent. A teacher interviewed during a study of disruptive pupils in Sheffield (Galloway *et al.* 1982) gave a vivid description of incidents which had persuaded her that there was no point in seeking help because none would be given. She told her interviewer:

Quite honestly, I tend not to refer kids for disruptive behaviour [to the Senior Staff] if I can help it. It involves me in more hassle than its worth. There's no trust in the relationships involved [i.e. between the speaker and her senior colleagues] . A number of kids have been put in the special group for disruptive pupils or have been sent out of the school for swearing at the deputy − but if it is one of us it happens to, nothing is done. When I informed the Head of a boy being rude to the school nurse, nothing was done. When he saw a similar incident several months later, the boy was excluded at once.

A similar problem was raised by a teacher in one of my interviews:

I felt very little support when dealing with major discipline problems − including assault.

These teachers would have been glad of the support of decisive actions by Head and senior staff but my reports also suggest that there are many occasions in school when teachers are not helped by their Head's decisive behaviour, if it is also autocratic. This kind of behaviour has a number of manifestations which include refusing to delegate decision making and authority, often because of the claim that the Head has ultimate responsibility which cannot be shared. This style of leadership also relies only minimally on consultation and emphasises the importance of what has been called 'initiating structure' in which the Head defines the roles he expects each teacher to assume by, for example, writing their job descriptions; establishes the aims of the school; and promotes the policies which in his opinion are necessary to achieve these goals. He pays little attention to 'consideration' which is respect and concern for the individual needs and interests of the members of staff (Bone 1983).

Some of the negative aspects of autocratic behaviour have been identified by the teachers in my groups. From the closeness of a Deputy's position in a comprehensive school an experienced teacher observed his Head's behaviour:

After a period of time attempting to put forward my own ideas without success and discovering that an unpleasant scene could arise from any initiative action which had not been given his minute scrutiny, one tended to fulfil one's administrative function mechanically and competently and concentrate on the teaching aspects of one's career which was a negative solution. One felt resentful of being excluded and not gaining essential experience. In retrospect I wonder if I should have persisted in my own viewpoint in the initial stages of this post, but whereas this may work with tact and diplomacy with some Heads, I do not consider in this case it would.

The non-consulting aspects of autocratic leadership behaviour were identified by a group of teachers in a staff development conference as a major problem:

We felt that the Headmaster should take certain decisions but we would like most of his decisions to be taken after consultation with his staff. We felt that we were presented with a *fait accompli* without any consultation. Consultation, we agreed, could not take place with everybody for every decision but we felt that it should take place between the Head and the people likely to be affected. We should be consulted, our views heard and respected, even if in the end they are rejected.

These organisational pressures and the financial and physical problems which were discussed earlier in this chapter may occur simultaneously and make a school an unhealthy place in which to work. This conclusion is supported by research which has shown a connection between unfavourable emotional and psychological factors in an organisation and the development of stress. These results provide considerable support for the conclusion that poor working conditions are significant sources of frustration, anger, anxiety and fear (Dunham 1976a).

6 THE PRESSURES ON THE TOP MANAGEMENT TEAM

The last chapter was concerned with the pressures exerted by Heads and Deputies on staff. In the present chapter I shall be discussing the demands experienced by the top management team. Teachers may be unaware of these problems and their criticisms of the leadership behaviour of senior management, in my experience, are often based upon a surprising degree of ignorance of the pressures exerted on Heads and Deputies. These include visits from angry parents, complaints from angry teachers and disruptive behaviour from angry pupils. Pressures from the media focus on the Head and are increasing. Legal requirements have become more complex recently and the increase in administrative paperwork is described in Heads' reports to me as a major burden. Increased expectations for accountability have already led to the introduction of time-consuming staff review procedures. The tasks of headship for which Heads are often untrained include elements of negotiating, controlling, directing, punishing, accounting, planning, counselling, healing and reviewing.

The tasks involved in the Deputy Head's role are very difficult to catalogue in this way because the range of expectations varies so much from school to school. At one end of this range is a structured role description which is exemplified as Deputy Head (Curriculum) or Deputy Head (Pastoral). At the other end there may only be a vague job description where the role approximates to that of a personal assistant to an executive. If this role ambiguity follows a period of structure and reasonable clarity of aims as a Head of Department, the adjustment required to be effective in the Deputy Head's role is considerable and may be only poorly appreciated by the staff who may have little time or enthusiasm to be concerned with the problems of the top management team. The identification of these pressures is a major task of this chapter and I want to start with the sources of work stress for Heads.

Headteachers

In the last five years, there have been a number of reports of increasing demands being made on Heads. This was contrary to the expectations of those Heads who believed that experience would make their work problems easier to resolve. One of them, a Head of a primary school, explained his difficulties because his previous experience did not provide the necessary coping methods:

> In recent times the pressures seem to have increased. When one is a new head one expects worries and problems but as time goes on, it is assumed, the job becomes slightly easier as experience comes to one's aid. Unfortunately this is not so. I find increasing pressures from the Authority (mainly because of continuing new legislation), constant changes in the curriculum and the ever-present demand to meet more and more deadlines. All these are additional to the pressures which have always been part of the job, e.g. standards, discipline, being the 'buffer' between staff and parents at times, child conduct, safety, etc. In other words, overall responsibility for all that goes on in a school. One of the problems dealing with stress is trying to 'switch off' out of school. I try not to take work home with me as much as possible and I live well away from the school and town. Worries are not too easy to leave behind.

Other Headteachers report that they feel stress when 'things are getting on top of them' because 'little hassles' which individually could be tackled effectively occur simultaneously to form a crisis (Lazarus 1981). For Heads of primary schools these crises might be the result of a number of events occurring during the same day, such as: absent staff; teachers who for various reasons are unable to cope; children with behaviour problems which need urgent attention; parents with urgent complaints; a breakdown in supplies (e.g. heating or food); and teaching commitments. The Headmaster of a secondary school gave an example of difficult situations which occurred simultaneously: a wet lunchtime in school exam week; a difficult parent arriving to see the Head; an angry caretaker because of what happened in the previous night's disco; a bus strike during external examinations; a fire alarm test; a defunct boiler in the staffroom; lack of ventilation in overflowing toilets; and teaching commitments.

Headteachers have also identified a number of problems as stress situations because individually they are severe enough to cause continuing, heavy pressures. Those reported include: parents' behaviour; staff behaviour; cuts in expenditure; pressures from the LEA; media pressures; union activities; and individual children's problems.

The behaviour of parents is a source of pressure for Heads in a number of ways. They report that they spend a disproportionate amount of time in dealing with parents whose children are in conflict with one another. The Head of a primary school gave me an example of this kind of problem:

At a time when pupil violence against teachers is receiving much publicity, I am grateful to be able to report that this is not a stress with which I am faced. However, I would say that violence between children is, on occasion, one of the most worrying aspects of the modern school and I have been involved in dealing with such incidents. Some children just seem incapable of realising the harm that they could do to others. We have had incidents that included the spiteful throwing of stones, attempted strangling, biting and kicking. Fortunately, in the majority of cases, the parents have been helpful in backing the school, but in some unfortunate cases the parents have been singularly unhelpful and positively antagonistic towards the staff. There was one incident in which teachers saw an incident involving kicking, but even then the parents refused to accept the situation and accused the teachers of lying and having a vendetta against their child. This was, in fact, dealt with by direct confrontation with the parents and the sheer weight of evidence. In another incident where a child had attacked another, the teacher on duty had to haul the attacker off and was unfortunately injured in the process. Treatment is still going on. The procedure now is that in the event of such happenings, my presence is immediately called for on the playground. I can't say this bothers me too much as the incidents are relatively infrequent, but there is always the nagging concern that perhaps something could go drastically wrong.

Parental pressures also evoke other strong emotions in Heads, for example when their schools are in multi-ethnic and disadvantaged inner-city areas. The parents of children in these schools have enormous problems and when they come into school they often seek help from the Headteacher. When the help which can be offered is inadequate, feelings of anxiety, helplessness and depression are experienced. The children's problems are major sources of stress for Heads for two reasons. They want to give support to a teacher who is finding the classroom situation very difficult to manage and they become directly involved in helping the children. Outside agencies which include Social Services, police, Department of Health and Social Security officials and probation officers have responsibilities for these families and Heads' workloads are increased by trying to overcome barriers to effective interprofessional communications with these workers (Dunham 1980b). If there is a sense of failure because little has been achieved, and if there is a sense of guilt at the amount of time spent on one child's problems, the stress factor is increased.

Parental behaviour which also causes Heads to experience considerable worry and frustration is concerned with husband–wife relationships. This happens when parents' interviews about pupils' progress in school become marriage guidance consultations for which Heads are not trained and usually have little experience. One example of this kind of problem is the mother who asks to see the Head about her child but during the interview seeks the advice of the Head about her plans to separate from her husband.

Parental pressures are also related to their increasing expectations of playing a greater part in the work and management of the school. These changing expectations have led to an increase in questions asked by parents about the aims and authority of the school. The Head of a primary school suggested an interesting explanation for these increasing demands:

> Parents are now thoroughly upset by the media and particularly by the reports of 'a lack of basics' in school and by the discussions of the likelihood of school leavers not getting jobs. These worries are exacerbated by their own financial problems.

Pressures from parents and pressures from the media are becoming more closely related. Articles published in the press have presented parents with lists of questions to ask Heads. The use of these lists have resulted in demands for information about the Heads' qualifications and educational values and even the state of the toilets.

A different but still difficult media pressure was reported by the Head of a comprehensive school:

> The public criticism in the local newspaper two years ago caused a great deal of stress for my staff and myself. It arose through the appointment as a governor of the School of a parent who had transferred his child to another school. This was reported with some derogatory comments by the paper and was followed by several weeks of letters for and against the school, encouraged by the paper. I was in fact away on a year's secondment at the time but I reacted

very strongly with a mixture of intense anger and anxiety — as did many of the staff — perhaps because of our helplessness to do anything about it.

These media comments on education which demand higher standards of pupil achievement and teacher performance have additional consequences. One of the most significant is that teachers feel undervalued by their local community and in the whole country.

These feelings of being undervalued are I think reinforced by the contraction in the Education Service which Heads have experienced. One important aspect is the capitation allowance allocated to schools which means that severe pressures occur when Heads find it impossible to satisfy all the demands by their staff for a share of the available money. In order to satisfy the requirements of the academic departments the money originally allocated to furniture and fittings may have to be spent and then no funds are available to prevent schools becoming shoddy.

Contraction has also resulted in the reduction of staff in schools because of falling rolls. One major consequence in primary schools has been the acceptance by the Head of the responsibilities of full-time class teacher. The implications of this change are clearly outlined by the Head of an infant school:

This Infant School has been reduced in number from 278 to 79 i.e. a reduction from *10 full-time staff to 3*. The cuts in teaching staff caused me to decide to teach a class full-time. The problems caused by my teaching commitment are:
(a)   Lack of contact with parents who normally are welcome to call any time.
(b)   Interruptions causing the disruption of my class and a lack of continuity in my teaching.
(c)   Inability to teach other classes and get to know the children.
(d)   Inability to visit other classes while the teachers and children are working.
(e)   Difficulty in discussing problems with staff because of lack of time in catching up with administration, messages, telephone calls, etc.
(f)   Not enough time to give visiting students, in-service training, etc.
(g)   Stress of constantly being aware of areas which need attention and yet being unable through lack of time, energy or the

demands of one's class to deal with them.
(h) Various problems have also been caused by the deterioration in the standard of repairs of the building which is over 100 years old and the increase in administrative work required. However, the reductions in staffing and the necessity to teach full-time has caused much greater problems.

I have had more absence from school during the last year than at any time for six years. I had influenza, laryngitis, whooping cough and spondylosis.

Contraction has also meant reduced opportunities for personal and professional growth. Appointment to a headship would usually be associated with expectations of change and progress not with decline. But the following report from the Head of a middle school shows how great was the difference between optimistic anticipation and harsh experience:

The cuts in educational spending started just as I became a Head so my time was spent preserving existing ideas and standards rather than being creative and expanding educational ideas. Staff cuts meant a lack of flexibility so that a minor crisis had a knock-on effect and disrupted many plans. The long-term plans kept having to be scrapped because the cuts were never known about until the last moment. The County did not appear to have any concern for the welfare of new Heads.

Similar comments have been made by other Heads about the behaviour of their LEA officials. They claim that in dealing with their Authority they have had to be very patient and they must be prepared to accept that what they consider to be urgent for their school will not receive the attention by the County officials which the situation requires. The Head of a primary school gave further details of these problems:

I feel that a lot of stress is caused by requests to County Hall not being dealt with promptly, no acknowledgement of requests or reasons for delay, thus incurring too many unnecessary letters and telephone calls to chase up things which should have been dealt with without any reminder being necessary. The School Governors, the PTA and myself have been fighting for the provision of an extra Temporary Classroom for the last two years, when it was first promised. Class 2 teacher's stress was relieved when the new class-room came into use at the beginning of this term. If this classroom had been erected a year earlier, life would have been less stressful for that classteacher and myself, as apart from the interruptions caused by the delay and the erection of the classroom we were both 'bulg-ing at the seams' as far as numbers were concerned.

Another kind of LEA pressure was experienced by the Head of a primary school. He is an NUT member and has supported his staff when they have withdrawn voluntary services during union action. His involvement caused him to feel a deep sense of conflict and stress. The threat of legal action by the LEA during one withdrawal of supervisory duties made him very angry at the officials' lack of support and non-understanding of his distress.

For other Heads for whom union action has been a possibility and a reality on a number of occasions there has been a similar conflict of loyalties between the children's safety, the task of manning the school, the support of teachers in their professional claims for adequate work-ing conditions and pay and the parents' wishes.

The Head of a high school found the behaviour of some of his staff during one union action particularly distressing:

I find the assertive Union presence a further stress area — but then who doesn't these days? The memory of some staff walking out during period eight because of a Union directive remains a bitter moment of shame and despair.

The behaviour and attitudes of teachers are major sources of stress for Heads for several reasons in addition to union actions. Four major problems can be identified from the written and oral information which Heads have given me. These are: incompetent staff; staff who are un-adaptable; staff who disturb their colleagues; and teachers whose atti-tudes to school management create long-standing difficulties.

Heads' definitions of incompetence include poor teaching ability which is so inadequate that it is very difficult to decide which children should go in their classes because they suffer for a year. Teachers are also described as incompetent when their general standard of work is unacceptably low to all their colleagues but not to themselves.

The Head of a first school gave a specific example of the difficulties she and her colleagues experienced from incompetent teacher be-haviour. It was in the form of a question to me:

How do I 'encourage' a weak member of staff, who does not appear to organise her class or teaching methods. The children regress emotionally and socially after transferring to her class and other members of staff have made it known that they are reluctant to pass their children on to her at six years as they feel much of their work is wasted. Colleagues have tried to help the teacher by discussion and by encouraging her to visit other classes, but the teacher is not prepared to change her approach to teaching. It was suggested that she taught an older age range but she replied that she will move when it suits her. The situation has been like this for about three years and has created a very bad atmosphere at school.

Teachers who are unadaptable are common causes of frustration and anger. Their resistance to change can be seen in their attitudes to the introduction of less formal approaches to teaching and in their attitudes to such matters as changes in disciplinary procedures. When staff are very reluctant to become involved in ways of working which are different from those they have used for many years, they present major problems for Heads who wish to implement curricular and organisational development in their schools. These are exacerbated if Heads feel under strong expectations from their LEA to innovate, e.g. to develop team teaching in open-plan primary schools, if they are newly appointed and if the 'resisters' are senior members of staff.

These factors can be identified in the following report:

The staff are in a rut with attitudes of non-co-operation and silent militancy. It is an old primary school. Several of them have been at the school for nearly twenty years. They are nearly all secondary trained. The Head, whose retirement caused the vacancy I filled, had organised the staffing so that the three male teachers always took the top classes and the female deputy resentfully took the top stream of the Third Year class. It was a very formal situation with the main emphasis on the Three Rs. There was coaching in the dinner hours for external examinations. When I became Head the Deputy immediately started pushing for changes which she considered were long overdue and which included team teaching and family grouping. At the beginning of my second year I changed the staffing to implement these changes. There was a lot of resistance and I thought at one stage that the older teachers would refuse to comply. When the changes were made they found it very difficult to cope with the younger or less able children. The staff relationships were awful.

The staff management difficulties reported in this school as a corollary of innovation have been found in different circumstances in other schools. Heads who wanted to encourage more participation by staff in significant decision making within the school, because they believed that this style of management encouraged staff involvement, enthusiasm and commitment, have sometimes been frustrated by non-co-operation and lack of initiative by even senior members of staff.

This problem was discussed by the Headmaster of one of the early comprehensive schools who wrote of his disappointment that open discussion did not produce the consensus of opinion that he had hoped for as a basis for decision making (John 1972). It frequently resulted in a wide divergence of recommendations with the result that the teachers became exasperated with discussion and disillusioned with participation and consultations.

In 1982 one of my informants in a primary school described a similar experience:

> The staff have either been reticent or have had such widely diverging views that it has been difficult to reach a decision without appearing autocratic. I have now concluded that I must have a definite proposal ready in case of difficulties and attempt to get the staff's nominal approval. This may fail to get their enthusiastic support as it does not come from them and it gives them the opportunity to criticise it as it has been presented to them from above. I am of the opinion that some staff enjoy being directed in an autocratic way and also enjoy the opportunity presented to criticise the situation they are then in.

And since 1982 there are signs that this type of management difficulty for Heads is increasing as their reports suggest that some teachers are becoming resentful at being given certain responsibilities on the assumption that they are an integral part of staff duties. They are now seeking more formal definitions of duties in which the distinction between contractual and voluntary is articulated without ambiguity. Their ultimate aim appears to be that all duties outside actual classroom teaching must be paid for as additions to salary.

There is one other aspect of staff attitudes and behaviour which will probably also make increasing demands on Headteachers' management skills. These are the problems caused by disappointed staff, some of which can be identified in the following report from a Head of a primary school:

The Deputy hoped to take over as Head when I was appointed but was not even considered. She has since said she bears no personal grudge to me for being appointed but feels very badly treated by the authorities after her long service. She is soon now to retire herself but it has taken five years of patient understanding and some stand-up arguments and mutual disagreements for us to build up a working relationship. The Deputy prides herself on being brutally frank with me and all members of staff and this gives rise to some conflict in the staffroom, when the frankness is either unjust or tactless or too near the truth for comfort. 'Pouring oil on troubled water' is my method of dealing with this stress situation, taking some of the 'smarting' out of the open wound, but I am not sure it is always right. My trouble is in keeping my relationship right with the Deputy. I have tried open discussion on subjects causing conflict and stress but this is not always successful and it seems better to keep an 'open door' for people to pour out their problems and conflicts to me (preferably with the Deputy present — but this has not been possible often enough) and trying to find mutual solutions and how best to avoid misunderstandings.

Deputy Heads

This is an interesting and clear description of the problems presented to a Head by the behaviour of her Deputy and some of the attempts she made to improve staff relationships in school. But I would have liked to hear more about the Deputy's feelings of disappointment and anger when she was not appointed to the headship and the pressures she experienced after the disappointment. At this time she might have needed extra support to deal with these circumstances as well as the 'ordinary' pressures of the Deputy's role.

These pressures can be divided into three main groups:

(a)   A wide range of responsibilities.
(b)   Role conflict.
(c)   Difficult relationships with Head, staff, pupils and parents.

There is a wide range of tasks in the role of Deputy from the very trivial to the very important. There are urgent, unplanned situations requiring instant attention, for example a parent or a pupil or a colleague in distress. The range of work for some deputies includes coping with staff absences; trying to improve the performance of poor teachers and motivating those who are running out of hope of promotion; controlling disruptive pupils and trying to motivate those pupils who, because of a high incidence of unemployment in the catchment area of the school, believe that school achievement is irrelevant to their future; and teaching a considerable number of lessons on a regular basis. The extensive and elastic nature of the role is perhaps best seen when there is no job description and the Deputy is told by the Head that the development of the job is dependent on his or her personality, experience and skills. But the existence of a job description is no guarantee that the post holder will have an accurate perception of the boundaries of the job. There are extension clauses built into job descriptions as the following example from a Deputy in a secondary school illustrates:

The official version of my job description when appointed, is shown below:

Oversight and co-ordination of the administration of the school.
Preparation of the timetable.
Arrangements for staff cover.
Staff duties and staff welfare.
Oversight of the pastoral care structure in the school.
Production of the monthly staff circular and the minutes of the various Year Heads' and Department Heads' meetings.
Membership of several school and PTA committees.
Responsibility for in-service training and for probationary teachers.
Press liaison and general public relations.
School discipline.

The job description also included the statement:

This list is intended to be no more than a guide to the deputy's duties. The successful candidate must have the necessary ability and energy to become involved in all aspects of the school and to make a significant contribution to its continued development.

Another job description showing only a small number of similar responsibilities with this one was provided by a Deputy in a comprehensive school:

Much of the responsibility of the Head on his absence. Overall day to day responsibility for the boys' welfare and discipline (particularly with regard to the Upper School).

Responsibility (with the Head) for curriculum innovation and planning.

The construction of the timetable.

A co-ordinating role with both Year Heads and Departmental Heads; also any other staff advisory groups to bring matters to the attention of the Head and help frame school policy.

Responsibility for daily substitution (in consultation with another Deputy Head).

Responsibility for the engagement of supply teachers.

Responsibility for the compilation of the academic calendar.

Responsibility for the planning of all external and internal examinations.

Responsibility for all arrangements concerned with visitors and the use of rooms.

Responsibility (with another Deputy Head) for First Aid.

A number of problems are associated with this wide range of expectations. Role conflict is one of the most serious and frequent. There are different kinds of conflict situations which put pressures on Deputies. One type occurs when the Deputy has a major teaching commitment as in the following report:

> My dual role as teacher and administrator causes stress. I teach a half-timetable and I find that my lessons are often interrupted by office staff and also by colleagues who either come themselves with problems or who send pupils to me when they feel that they cannot deal with them. I take my teaching seriously and I am very conscious of my duty to my pupils and my need to set a good example to my colleagues. I appreciate, on the other hand, that the teacher with a full timetable meets situations which need to be 'cooled down' immediately and that he feels his need is great. Some of the interruptions are obviously concerned with trivia, others, although at first appearing to be minor, have turned out to be serious.

Strong pressures also occur for Deputies when they attempt to reconcile conflicting interests in school which include those between pupil and pupil; pupil and member of staff; two teachers; members of staff and the Head; and between staff and parents.

There are conflicting interests between 'today' and 'tomorrow', that is between the demands of day-to-day work and the need for long-term planning. There is a similar conflict between the unpredictable crises of staff and pupils and the Deputy's own daily list of priorities. These problems often result in the major time pressures which are identified in my reports. One woman who said she was under severe stress wrote:

> I am literally pursued along corridors by staff. I have no breaks or lunch hour. My dinner consumption has been timed at 2 minutes 38 seconds by a colleague.

Conflict is reported because of uncertainty about other people's roles in the school and confusion about their areas of responsibility. This situation leads to considerable frustration and anxiety when the role of the Deputy Head is undefined in a school and role boundaries are unclear between members of the senior management team or between them and middle management. Some of the characteristics and effects of this type of conflict are identified in the following report, which is also interesting because of the writer's belief that it was created deliberately by the Head:

> Role conflict is the main stress area. The Senior Management Team has responsibility for Administration, Pastoral and Curriculum. The Head, Deputy Head (woman) and Senior Master 'float' around these areas. The Head (a recent appointment) believes in applying pressure by playing one person off against another to see how they will react. He fails to allow anyone to accept overall responsibility for their role and sometimes makes changes or decisions without even letting the team know. Added to this he also has been known to change his mind after pressure by a strong member of staff and tends to let small decisions become major conflicts in the staffroom.

These role conflict situations are closely connected with the third major area of pressure for deputies which is difficult relationships with the Head, teaching staff, parents, non-teaching staff and pupils.

Some of these problems occur when the people concerned interact with each other in disturbing confrontations and the Deputy becomes an intermediary or negotiator. A clear example of these difficulties was presented by a Deputy in a primary school. When she was appointed it soon became obvious to her that two members of staff were frustrated by their lack of communication between themselves and the Head. One was a young female teacher who was in her first appointment and had three years' experience. She felt unappreciated and she was frequently defensive ('I always do it this way'). Her discipline was very weak. The parents complained to the Head, who complained to the teacher who wept. The second teacher was a man with a scale 2 post who was lethargic and aggressive. His conversations with the Head usually became arguments which resulted in a loss of temper for both of them. The Deputy had to act as the confidante to both and calm them down. The Head also created problems when he was aggressive to any parent who disagreed with him.

The Deputy of another primary school also encountered difficulties in her relationships in school:

> I took over as Deputy Head, well aware of the problems I was to face. I had been warned by colleagues and advisers that the Head was an autocrat. This proved to be very true. As soon as I tried to make any decisions I was firmly put in my place. I also felt that certain members of the staff were hostile as they had wanted my post. It was lunch time that I found to be most trying — having to make polite conversation with the Head — with whom I had few interests in common. The pressures were increased by the fact that the previous Deputy had been a great friend of the Head and was still brought back to take part in concerts and go on school journeys, all of which made me feel rather inadequate. The symptoms of the stress took the form of severe headaches. I found that chocolate helped to bring them on. I have been able to restart eating chocolate since a new Head arrived at Christmas. I became very short tempered at home especially with my own children. To cope with the stress I comforted myself by thinking that he was due to retire soon. I spent a lot of time talking with two close friends and my wife, also by going sailing most weekends. The latter didn't stop the headaches, but did help put life into perspective.

Some of the relationship difficulties which Deputies in other schools report are related to the task of counselling the teachers who want to discuss their hopes and fears with a member of the senior management team. Some staff want a sounding board for their problems; others request a critical appraisal of their career prospects; a few need to cry and more want to complain; a growing number are seeking advice on job applications and interviews; and some have major personal and marital problems.

Many Deputies' reports indicate that these staff counselling pressures constitute a significant part of their workloads. The weight of these demands was clearly expressed by a Deputy in a secondary school:

> The most stressful situations are those where I am called upon to resolve stress or conflict in other people's relationships. Having said that it is important to add that I find this to be one of the more interesting and challenging elements of the job as well as that which generates the most stress.

The frustration and resentment which can be generated by these demands when they are not seen as challenging and interesting can be felt in the report of a Deputy Head:

> My pressures include having to cope with problems beyond the scope of my training. I am not a psychologist, nor a psychiatrist, nor a social worker, nor a marriage guidance counsellor.

This is a common complaint and it indicates an unwillingness to become involved in the development of pastoral care for teachers. This attitude of members of the senior management team has important implications for all members of staff because it limits the range of alternative sources of help which are available in school. But my work with Heads of Department and Pastoral Care Team Leaders suggests that these members of middle management are urgently in need of the support of top management because of the problems they experience. Their pressures are identified in the next chapter.

7 THE PRESSURES ON MIDDLE MANAGEMENT

The first part of this chapter is concerned with the demands generated by substantial changes in the role of Head of Department as it has developed in comprehensive schools. One major change has resulted in departmental heads becoming involved in management responsibilities for the work of the staff in their departments, while still being required to carry a heavy teaching programme. The second part of the chapter discusses the pressures on Pastoral Care Heads arising from their wide range of duties which includes being responsible for pupils' discipline, pupils' problems and liaison with external agencies as well as having to teach for much of the week. These multiple demands on Heads of House and Year also create major problems of role conflict and role confusion.

The Changing Role of Heads of Department in Comprehensive Schools

The change in the role of departmental heads in comprehensive schools is an important area for investigation: there is a sharp contrast between the post in grammar and comprehensive schools. The managerial aspects of a Head of Department's role in a grammar school may involve little more than ordering books for the department once a year. When a grammar school is reorganised into a comprehensive the role may change so much that it may be misleading to retain the same name for it. A department is now responsible for several different levels of teaching. There is a much wider range of pupil behaviour, motivation and attitudes and the training, skills and expectations of staff are more variable. The person in the post of departmental head now has an amplified role, in which extra duties and responsibilities have to be fitted into a full teaching schedule. There is very little provision made in school time for the many jobs connected with the management of a department. The resulting loss of effectiveness can be considerable.

Several types of demands, which have resulted from these curricular and organisational changes, can be identified in the following report by a Head of Department in a comprehensive school:

Most stress is experienced outside the classroom, in the numerous and multiplying chores which seem so inevitable in the running of a large school. I dream of a school where all this fiddle-faddle and excessive paperwork have been dispensed with, so that I can spend much more time on the things I really want to do, i.e. running my department and teaching my pupils. This bumf seems to multiply day by day and I hate it.

Instability in my subject is another source of stress. Recent years have seen a surfeit of 'educationalists' messing about with subject material and generally making it less relevant, and often much less interesting to the pupils. 'New' Maths has been followed by 'New' Geography, and other subjects seem to be becoming increasingly afflicted. Such changes cause two kinds of problems. They sometimes mean that we are teaching material for which we have no respect, and the material and techniques at which we are expert are suddenly (and often in our view wrongly) condemned as obsolete and boring. Quite often we feel that the reverse is true. The second problem is the very practical one of 're-tooling' with new and expensive books which themselves may be considered obsolete when the next bright idea comes down to us from above. I used to know where I stood with regard to the school, the educational system and my subject. Now I often feel I am standing on quicksand.

The pressures of having to perform 'numerous and multiplying chores' against the background of a major teaching commitment can be clearly seen in the report of a head of a science department:

I teach 34 periods (out of 40) each week. I make a practice of teaching actively rather than letting pupils work on their own while I do something else. My subject involves a lot of experimental work and supervision is necessary for safety. This means that all additional work must be done in 'free time' and outside school. This work includes marking books, setting and marking examination papers, writing reports and testimonials, stock checking, ordering supplies and new apparatus, arranging for apparatus maintenance, tracing missing equipment and various other tasks. Contrary to popular belief, this can lead to a working week of 45–55 hours and I become tired. The planning of courses for less able pupils and control of unruly pupils can cause additional stress which may be considerable. Towards the end of term, my patience suffers and great self-control is needed to avoid confrontations with difficult pupils. At this stage it becomes difficult to 'switch off' and this can lead to further fatigue and feelings of frustration.

These reports suggest that increased administrative responsibilities are now an integral part of the role of Head of Department in a comprehensive school. But the management of a department has important relationship aspects and my informants indicate that interaction with colleagues can be a major source of stress. The difficult behaviour, indifferent attitudes and incompetence of staff create considerable problems for their Head of Department, particularly if there is a lack of time to keep a careful check on what every member of the department is teaching. Problems arise when a department is mainly composed of young first- and second-year teachers who may need a lot of guidance, especially when most of them are tackling examination work for the first time. The members of the department who fail to pull their weight; or cannot keep good discipline in their classes; or have low academic and professional skills; or are the subjects of complaints by pupils, parents and staff bring extra worry and work. The lack of initiative and ambition in staff; their lack of co-operation; their lack of effort; and their resistance to change are responsible for the development of considerable levels of frustration. There is also the problem of continuity when the levels of staff turnover and absenteeism are high.

Some of these problems of staff management can be recognised in the following questions asked by members of one of my university in-service courses for middle managers in secondary schools:

1. How do you re-motivate teachers who have lost interest in their jobs and who have not kept in touch with recent developments in the subjects they teach?
2. How do you improve the relationships between different teachers within the department which are strained at the moment because of conflicts of personality, lack of resources and shared rooms?
3. How do I help teachers who are afraid of being unpopular and of any sort of confrontation?

These departmental management pressures are increased when the Head of Department becomes involved in the interaction between departmental staff and pupils, parents, ancillary staff, other teachers and members of the senior management team. The role conflict and frustration which is experienced because of these problems of relationships is clearly expressed in the following descriptions of a difficult member of staff:

> One cause of stress to me is a member of my faculty. He is an excellent drama teacher — very gifted. His philosophy of the subject is admirable, his abilities unquestionable. He is *very* charming when he wants to be but he has an extraordinary way of upsetting other members of staff. I could describe some of the things he has done but it would take too long. However, I do get quite a lot of come-back from other members of staff. Most of the complaints are about things he doesn't do . . . paperwork . . . supervise children who are supposed to be with him at breaks . . . reports on time . . . etc., etc. and my problem is how to tell him tactfully and still keep a good working relationship with him. Any hint of real criticism is liable to make him lose his cool. Neither does he react very well to women teachers particularly in senior positions. It has taken me a couple of years to establish a position of trust and it's only now beginning to work properly. This is because he is working with a temporary replacement for his assistant who is away on maternity leave and he has made an excellent relationship with her replacement.

Role conflict also occurs for the Head of Department as he acts as an intermediary between his own department and others in the school or with the house or year heads. The Head of Department is required to act as a negotiator and this leads to feelings of vulnerability in 'boundary' situations when there is disagreement about the respective areas of responsibility. One said:

> I feel that you have to be rather a diplomat. I find that other Heads of Department are very, very sensitive when they think that anyone else is encroaching on their department. Some of them are very set in their ways and refuse to recognise any form of change when discussions on curriculum development are held.

The Head of Department may also experience role conflict in opening or maintaining channels of communication between teachers in the department and the senior management team. Staff may want their departmental head to put their point of view to the Head and Deputies or, if they are inexperienced, they may need reassurance when they communicate with the Head and Deputy Heads whom they see as authority figures.

Heads of Departments experience other kinds of problems in their dealings with senior management. The leadership behaviour of Head-teachers has been indicated by my informants as a major source of stress. Their reports suggest that serious difficulties are caused by several facets of Heads' management styles including: their reluctance to delegate any responsibility for decision making; a lack of communication between Head and Head of Department; the failure of a Head to appreciate the needs of individual departments which results in bad timetabling; the failure to provide clear job descriptions for Heads of Departments and their colleagues; the inability to provide a clear style of decision making; the appointment of staff without departmental consultation; the introduction of significant curricular changes without the participation of the departmental head; making timetable changes for staff without reference to the Head of Department; and finally the 'whittling away' of a department because of the Head's negative opinion about the importance of the subject.

The identification of these pressures caused by role conflict and increased administrative responsibilities provides strong, contemporary support for the conclusions of a Headmaster who wrote an innovatory analysis of the effects of changes in the role of Head of Department:

Leading a department in a large comprehensive school is, one must admit, very exhausting. The total number of hours involved and the total quantity of energy used are very high indeed. The sheer pressures of decisions required and initiatives to take will surprise the teacher who moves from a tripartite school system, and often, indeed, the new appointment who has had previous experience in a less senior post in a comprehensive school. The priorities are difficult to establish and there is continuous tension in the Head of Department's task – arguably more than in the post of Head-teacher (Marland 1971).

This review was important because it helped post holders and those teachers who were intending to apply for these posts to develop an objective awareness of the changing characteristics of the Head of Department's job.

Heads of House or Year

My aim in this chapter has also been to provide an up-to-date analysis which would stimulate an awareness of the onerous nature of departmental responsibilities. I have the same aim in my discussion of the middle management role of Head of House or Head of Year. I believe that these appointments often carry very heavy pressures in the comprehensive school organisation and if the people appointed are to meet those demands effectively the different components of their workload must be identified. My analysis suggests that the major problems are: multiplicity of tasks; too much work of a crisis management nature; teaching responsibilities versus pastoral care commitments; teamwork problems; poor communication with senior management team, colleagues and outside agencies; role conflict because of contradictory expectations of pupils, staff and parents.

The pressures arising from the multiplicity of tasks in the role were clearly noted by a Head of Year who gave me an itemised report of his job description. The routine duties included:

1. Liaison with Middle Schools and allocation of pupils to forms in collaboration with the School Counsellor.
2. Collection and collation of subject teachers' assessments of pupils' work at prescribed intervals.
3. Follow-up of problems revealed by assessments, by investigation involving individual pupils, subject teachers and form teachers concerned.
4. Instituting or responding to communication with parents of pupils with work or behaviour problems, by interview, letter or telephone.
5. Keeping records of assessments, copies of reports, testimonials, examination results and all other matters of importance to the welfare present and future of the pupils.
6. Arranging for the compilation of testimonials for pupils applying for places at institutions of further education or requested by prospective employers.
7. Monitoring the progress and behaviour of the forms within the year group, drawing to the attention of the Counsellor any serious problems arising within any form group.
8. Organising the weekly Year Assembly.
9. Keeping the form teachers and the pupils fully informed of all developments of importance to them.
10. Co-ordination of the work of the form teachers of the Year Group.
11. In-service training of inexperienced form teachers and helping

form teachers experiencing difficulties.

12. Supervision of the arrangements for the weekly form period.
13. The arranging of cover for absent form teachers.
14. Arranging for the sending to parents of unexplained absence forms.

This list illustrates the wide range of demands which may be experienced as the leader of a pastoral care team. But it does not show that much of the work is 'fire fighting', i.e. attempting to cope with a number of very urgent demands which need attention immediately. This crisis management aspect of the role can be seen in the following chronological recording of one school day of a Head of House. He insisted that it was an 'ordinary' day!

My day:
8.20   Put out chairs and hymn books for assembly.
8.40   Write some letters.
9.00   Assembly — visiting speaker. Dismiss approx. 500 pupils on my own.
9.30   See four pupils about incident in lesson on Monday — total breakdown with a very good teacher.
9.40   *Lesson.*
10.25 Break — go to see tutor of the four pupils.
10.40 *Lesson.*
11.15 *House Period.* Phone call from Senior Social Worker about two pupils. See tutor of the pupils.
11.50 *Lunch* with the four pupils.
12.40 Do some reports.
1.00   See teacher who had the problem with the four pupils.
1.30   On way to lesson 5th Year girl asks to see me urgently — not in my House. Talks to me.
1.45   Go to Headmaster concerning pupil.
2.00   Teacher sees me regarding written comments by pupil in an exercise book. Fail to get to lesson.
2.20   *Break* — see tutor to report on lunch session with four pupils.
2.40   *Lesson* arrive ten minutes late for film. Handed a letter saying no one will take a sick child to hospital. Teacher tells me about one of the girls in the House who has a problem. After film go with my group for discussion. Group increased from 19 to 27 due to member of staff being ill. Session lacks response from

pupils. I have to talk – not too well prepared – run out of time – but still a reasonable session.

3.40 Two pupils for detention.

4.45 Work to clear up.

6.15 Arrive home.

This recording of what was claimed to be a typical day also shows another source of stress – the conflict between pastoral care and teaching commitments. The latter include being part of the cover system for absent teachers resulting in the loss of non-teaching periods which had been planned for pastoral work.

There is often insufficient time to deal with the problems that arise and the pastoral team head may experience feelings of guilt because of missing meetings or having to go late to lessons, or perhaps missing them altogether when parents or outside agencies or children need his or her attention.

The next major problem to be identified is concerned with the teamwork difficulties which arise when subject teachers are unwilling to accept their pastoral care commitments. A good example of this kind of hassle was sent to me by a Head of House:

I have been a housemaster for five years, taking over a house from two previous housemasters. Four of the house staff are relatively new, whilst two have been tutors in the house from the beginning (ten years). My problem is with one of these: a formidable character, five years my senior, head of a department and very single minded. His attitude when I started as Housemaster was 'Here we go again, another new broom, lets make life as difficult as possible for him.' However, as the years have passed he has mellowed and I have become a little more patient and less demanding. I have had my little successes, getting him to do the odd assembly and accompany us on a house visit, etc. However, there are still times when he can be most obstructive and belligerent. This year he has been very involved with 16+ exams, which take up a lot of his time and energy. Hence the normal tutor chores of registration and general administration tend to get him down. Often I get the backlash of his vitriolic tongue. He wants to be relieved of tutor duties and objects to the general extra-curricular material he is expected as a tutor to collate. My initial response has been calm acknowledgement of his problems and a deliberate attempt to ease his burden. However, I feel I should not have to compromise my objectives of continuity within the house for the sake of the 16+ exam.

Teamwork difficulties for the team leader are exacerbated when there is ambiguity about the authority which goes with the job or about the place of the Pastoral Care Heads in the school's management structure. In these circumstances conflict can occur in such areas as the collection of subject teachers' assessments and the use of the form periods for planned tutorial work, such as the Lancashire County Council (1980) Active Tutorial Work syllabus and materials, when the subject teachers are dilatory or indifferent to their pastoral care responsibilities. The team leader can also be under pressure from other members of the team to give advice, provide information and to offer help.

Demands on the Head of House or Year are frequently related to matters of discipline, which range from the serious ones of physical and verbal violence to many trivial ones such as not wearing school uniform. These concerns become more frustrating when there are communication difficulties in which the members of the senior management team are involved. These occur when a teacher 'leapfrogs' the pastoral ladder and takes discipline problems straight to the Head or a Deputy without notifying the tutors or the team leader. These difficulties also occur when a Deputy and the Head do not pass on relative information about a pupil they have been concerned with to the pastoral system.

Communication difficulties, leading to considerable frustration and anger, also occur with professional child and family care agencies outside the school. These arise for several reasons. The children who are referred to the Head of House or Year by staff because they are disruptive or by parents because they are very difficult to control may also have come to the attention of the police, probation officers, Health and Social Services. Pupils who are having to tackle serious difficulties may need to be referred to an outside agency. A suspected pregnancy is an example of this type of situation.

The major causes of these interprofessional communication difficulties have been identified (Dunham 1981b). One of the major factors is the question of confidentiality which presents considerable problems for close professional co-operation. Social workers, child guidance staff and the medical services restrict effective communication with pastoral care staff when they are reluctant to share the contents of their files. One of the biggest worries of these professional workers is that if they give details of personal and family problems to pastoral care staff the information will soon become the gossip of the staffroom. Another major barrier to successful interaction with agencies outside the school is created when there is a rapid turnover of staff. This has been reported most frequently in the Social Services where it has caused problems in maintaining contacts with the social workers who are supervising pupils whom the pastoral care staff are attempting to help.

This brief discussion of some of the heavy demands arising from communication difficulties concludes this chapter on the problems found in middle management roles. It is also the end of the section of this book which aimed at identifying the pressures on all levels of staff. The next chapter is concerned with the important dimension of teachers' reactions to these pressures.

8 THE IDENTIFICATION OF STRESS REACTIONS

In this chapter, staff reactions to the pressures identified in the previous seven chapters will be grouped into four main categories: behavioural, emotional, mental and physical. These reactions will also be placed in a framework of successive stages which staff pass through as their work (and home) pressures become increasingly severe. In the first stage they develop new coping techniques or continue to use familiar strategies. If these coping actions are unsuccessful in reducing pressures, a number of emotional and mental reactions are experienced. These include frustration, anger, anxiety, fear, poor concentration and memory loss. Severe physical reactions develop when exposure to stress is prolonged. These include heart attacks, ulcers and skin disorders. Continued exposure to the stress situations identified in the previous chapters without a corresponding increase in coping resources brings fatigue, exhaustion and burn-out.

This framework is based on three theoretical perspectives which I have found helpful in understanding teachers' reactions to stress. The first theory identifies three stages: the alarm reaction, the stage of resistance and the state of exhaustion. The alarm is invoked when the inividual becomes aware of a stress situation. At this stage increased hormone secretions, including adrenalin, enter the bloodstream to help cope with the increased demands. If the demands are not reduced, the physiological responses, which may include changes in heart rate and pulse rate as well as hormone secretions, are maintained at a higher level than is normal for the individual in order to resist increasing demands. This strains and drains the body's resources. This could lead, for example, to a marked loss in body weight. Finally, if the stress continues, the body continues to draw on its deeper level of resources in a desperate attempt to cope. Exhaustion may be experienced at this stage, while prolonged exposure to severe stress may result in death (Selye 1956).

The second theory looks at the relationship, expressed in Figure 8.1, between the performance of the teacher's role and the demands which are experienced. In this theory, Hebb (1972) has proposed that work with only few demands leads to boredom. Increasing demands are regarded as stimulating and energising, but if they are beyond the person's coping abilities they lead to high levels of anxiety, poor

Figure 8.1: The Relationship Between the Teacher's Performance and the Demands Experienced

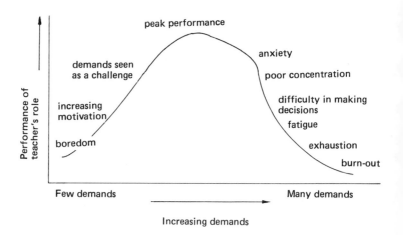

concentration and reduced effectiveness in one's work. Continued demands, without an increase in coping resources, may lead to fatigue, exhaustion and burn-out.

The third theoretical perspective which is helpful in understanding stress reactions also proposes that individuals pass through stress thresholds as they respond to increasing pressures. The first level consists of changes in behaviour which are used by the individual in an attempt to cope with new or increased demands. This is the 'new coping behaviour threshold'. If these attempts are unsuccessful in coping with the situation, the 'frustration threshold' is reached. If there is a continuing failure to cope, an individual may begin to question his competence and will experience strong feelings of anxiety. More severe disturbances may lead to the development of psychosomatic symptoms. As the individual uses up his coping resources he will reach and pass through the threshold of exhaustion (Appley 1967).

The initial response to pressures which are in excess of coping resources is, according to this theory, to try to use coping actions — for instance, to discuss the problem with colleagues. In this sense having to cope with difficulties is beneficial in that it promotes personal and professional development by stimulating the acquisition of additional patterns of behaviour and the strengthening of such personal resources as determination, self-control, tact, adaptability, calmness, patience and tolerance. The Head of Lower School in an inner-city comprehensive school provided a good example of this kind of growth when he wrote:

> This job made me much more tolerant at work than I would ever have believed possible.

Teachers' personal characteristics and coping actions are of considerable significance in tackling stress situations and they are discussed in detail in the next chapter. But the present chapter is concerned with the sequence of reactions when coping strategies are not effective and personal resources are becoming depleted.

Stage-by-stage Examination of the Stress Process

Frustration

The first reaction is frequently frustration which causes a wide range of feelings from irritation to angry aggression. Anger is not necessarily directed at the source of frustration as, for example, when it is the Headteacher's inconsistent leadership behaviour which is causing most of the hassles. In these circumstances anger would tend to be displaced to other targets. The following reports indicate two of these targets. First is one from a Senior Master:

> There is the likelihood of my carrying over the tension into the teaching situation so that the innocent suffer and of allowing the problems to carry over into non-school areas, so that they dominate life at home to the detriment of family relationships.

This second target, the teacher's family, was used by the Deputy Head of a comprehensive school. His wife asked me:

> Do you ever give a thought to the wives of teachers, who find themselves as whipping boys? There is more cruelty than physical cruelty you know and there comes a time when you can't take any more of the bitterness and frustration that always somehow find their way back to the wives of certain men under pressure. My life seems to be one long hell and the only time there is any relief is when there has been a row or blow up of some kind in school. Then I don't get the full brunt. My husband will not admit

to any suggestion that he needs to see a doctor. We are all wrong except him.

But the anger caused by frustration is not always expressed overtly either in direct or indirect channels. If it is 'bottled-up' for long periods there is a risk of psychosomatic symptoms such as headaches, stomach upsets, sleep disturbances, high blood pressure and skin disorders. A Deputy Head identified several of these reactions:

> In extreme cases I have headaches, stomach upsets and difficulty in sleeping — all caused, one supposes, by tensions. These never prevent me from attending school.

The relationship between suppressed anger and high blood pressure has been clearly presented by Buss (1961):

> When an individual becomes angry, his blood pressure rises. Since anger is a temporary reaction, the elevation in blood pressure is temporary. Some individuals inhibit the expression of anger and their rage subsides only slowly. They cannot cope with rage, failing to express aggression against those they blame. They remain tense and uncomfortable. As their blood pressure rises more often and stays high for longer periods it becomes a permanent condition.

Suppressed anger has also been reported by the same writer to be crucially involved in the development of some skin disorders. His studies have indicated that unexpressed rage is associated with an increase in the temperature of the skin. These skin changes tend to last longer because the individual is unable to discharge his pent-up tension by means of an outburst of aggression. Gradually the reddening of the skin does not disappear and is accompanied by an intense itching.

Anxiety

These different reactions to increasing frustration show several interesting comparisons to the next major emotional response to be discussed. This is anxiety. If feelings of being anxious are slight, teachers may experience a sense of stimulation and alertness which is pleasurable rather than stressful. Increasing demands or more rapid changes or a greater degree of role uncertainty about how a role should be enacted may initiate the arousal of higher levels of anxiety. These may be unproductive in the sense that a teacher's ability to make decisions is impaired or his ability to concentrate is reduced. There may be feelings of panic or an awareness of physiological changes such as accelerated heart rate, more rapid breathing and sweating palms. There may also be a sharp loss of confidence in teaching skills (Cherniss 1980). This reaction was noted by the Head of a primary school:

Conflicts between staff and pupils can undermine the self-confidence of the member of staff until he doubts whether he is able to cope at all. The difficulty is that this is a vicious circle: because he lacks confidence in his own abilities, he is less likely to handle the situation well. All young teachers and most teachers of all ages find themselves in this position from time to time.

Feelings of panic were identified by the Headteacher of another primary school:

Basically the times of stress have seemed to come in small waves. I tend to have a series of 'good' weeks when things go well and then a week of disasters. My immediate reaction when a crisis occurs is one of gut sinking panic, but this I have learnt to hide – I find that if I concentrate on one crisis at a time it helps, but often I feel like a juggler with too many balls to keep in the air!

There are important mental aspects of anxiety and some of these were referred to by the Head of a primary school:

I think stress can be distinguished through its effects of lack of sleep, anxious waking or waking very early and feelings of depression about work. Stress is most alarming when there is nothing to which it can be attributed and so once a source of stress is identified it immediately becomes less stressful.

When there is prolonged exposure to situations which cause anxiety, such as those characterised by uncertainty about one's future in an amalgamation of two schools or the closing of a single school, physiological changes occur which can lead to the appearance of psychosomatic symptoms. These anxiety-inducing situations are particularly potent in provoking a high rate of adrenalin secretion. The significance of this physiological change has been clearly stated by a research worker who has been interested for some years in the connection between unfavourable emotional and psychological factors in an organisation and the development of stress symptoms. His research results led him to the conclusion that:

> Anxieties, tensions and frustrations as well as sensory annoyance (especially noise) cause the release into the blood stream of adrenalin and other substances which may contribute towards the development of sudden heart attacks (Raab 1971).

Exhaustion

If the heavy demands on teachers continue there are frequent indications in their reports to me that they have reached the exhaustion threshold. These feelings of tiredness are different from those experienced after heavy work in the holidays. This is a particular type of tiredness which is often described as 'drained'. A teacher in a comprehensive school gave a very clear description of this condition:

> There was too much paper work and discussion which seemed fruitless. Nothing seemed resolved by the hours given up to the discussion and a feeling of frustration prevailed. It became a vicious circle. The workload was such that one was constantly feeling exhausted but because of a situation in the school that absenteeism caused an even heavier workload on colleagues, one was reluctant to take time off unless absolutely essential. This caused more exhaustion and stress, coupled with feelings of guilt that one was not doing the job as well as one might. Upholding standards, both in teaching and in the behaviour of pupils, seemingly without much support, was a constant strain. It would have been very easy to give up the struggle!!

Burn-out

If this level of exhaustion is not relieved by holidays or by absence from school through illness or by taking courses there is a real risk that it will become burn-out. In this condition which one teacher described as 'being a burnt out husk' teachers are completely drained – emotionally, physically, behaviourally, mentally, sexually and spiritually (Forney *et al.* 1982). Physical symptoms range from chronic exhaustion, low resistance to illness and alcoholism. Mental symptoms include a deep and impenetrable cynicism. Behavioural symptoms include chronic absenteeism and leaving teaching altogether. A teacher who was advised by his doctor to leave teaching and was given a medical disability pension wrote of the difficulties which eventually forced him to find different work:

> After ten years I was forced to give up teaching in spite of the tremendous enthusiasm I put into the work. The combination of late nights spent marking unwillingly-written exercises, disciplinary problems with non-academic teenagers, a phase under a weak headmaster who deluded himself that his pupils could do no wrong, and a final short-lived encounter with the rigours of a large progressive comprehensive school led me to seek the quieter life of an office job where I am at present rusting away.

The Headteacher of an infant school wrote:

> I have seen the stress which teachers experience when they expect a very high standard from very young children. I had one teacher of the reception class who suffered a nervous breakdown. No amount of reassurance, that she was doing fine, removed the stress she was feeling, and finally when she returned after about four weeks' absence, she was only able to teach small groups of children. Even the mention of her going into a class by herself would reduce her to tears. This teacher is now leaving infant teaching after two years at my school.

A teacher in a comprehensive school who had used all her coping resources and could not replenish them had stopped going to work in the middle of term and even with the help of her doctor she could not force herself to go back. The symptoms she described indicate the condition of burn-out:

> I have feelings of not achieving anything: it is pointless; I have feelings of depression; I have tension in my head; I have lost half a stone in three months; I switch from one decision to another — I will leave — No I won't; cannot switch my mind off; feelings of panic; I can't watch television; I thought I was going crazy; disturbed sleep and eating; I stopped going to meetings; I can't face going to school.

This brief discussion of burn-out completes the stage-by-stage examination of the stress process. Now I want to present details of stress reactions in terms of different groups of teachers. These are staff experiencing school closure; the staff in secondary schools who have used me as a stress consultant for their staff in-service training conferences; middle management team leaders; and Heads and Deputies.

Staff Experiencing School Closures

My work with the teachers coping with the closure of their school started when I was invited by the Head to be the consultant in their in-service training day. The theme of the day was 'Adapting to Change'. It took place just after the first half-term and was arranged to provide the staff with an opportunity to discuss ways of coping with the closure of their school at the end of the school year.

Before the conference I interviewed individually 12 members of staff. The main results of the interviews were given to the teachers during the in-service day and were discussed by them in small groups and in a plenary session. This report is a summary of my interviews and the group discussions with the 33 teachers who were on the school roll.

There were five major reactions to the closing of the school. These were the use of coping resources, anger, unwillingness to prepare for redeployment, anxiety and loss of confidence. The statements of the staff which are given below provide specific details of these reactions:

Use of Coping Resources
I have the inner strength of knowing that I have adapted before; I said to myself — Ah well there's more to life than teaching; Good reports seemed to have been given about me by the Head and my other referees and this gradually helped me to overcome my self-doubts; My fears of working in my new school are not great ones as I have taught in many schools; I have had a great deal of support from friends outside school; The staff in general have been marvellous and they have ignored my black moods on my bad days; In my new school I will use a number of survival strategies — don't rush your fences, know what the school is, know the opposition.
Anger
The anger which was expressed in the interviews and during the training day was strong and bitter. There were feelings of being let down by the Authority, which were made more intense for those teachers who felt they had betrayed the children's trust by not working hard enough to maintain the viability of a familiar and friendly school. Feelings of anger were increased by a sense of discrimination and even of stigma. The statements which expressed

these different aspects of anger included these three: I feel really let down by the LEA; I felt really angry at the Head; I felt discriminated against.

Unwillingness to Prepare for the Closing Down of the School at the End of the Summer Term

Two of these statements were: I will be all right; If I haven't got a job by Easter I will begin to worry then. This unwillingness-to-prepare reaction denied the need for concern at this point in the school year and questioned the relevance of a training day arranged for this purpose. Only a small minority of the staff expressed these attitudes.

Anxiety

Clear indications of the specific anxieties of staff are given in the following statements: My main worry has been about not getting an equal post; I am worried about the cost of moving home; I don't want to teach subjects for which I am not trained; I am apprehensive about the pupils' behaviour, uncaring attitudes and bad language in another school; I would hate to be in a situation where I could not cope; It's a frightening challenge; I will have to prove myself all over again in the new school; I shall have to build up a rapport with the children again; I am worried about being plonked on to another school.

Loss of Confidence

The statements indicating loss of confidence were: I have not needed to move around much so this is more of a shake-up; My adjustment will depend on other people's reactions to me; I realised I had interviewed badly; I felt rusty in my interview; I never failed an interview before.

The interviewing difficulties which are referred to by staff are important causes of their loss of confidence. They had not realised that their interviewing skills had become less effective and it was only when they went to talk to the Head of another school to discuss possible redeployment to that school, that they became aware of their poor performance. One teacher after this experience persuaded the Deputy to give him some mock interviews.

Check Lists of Staff Stress in Secondary Schools

These reports of coping actions and some of the mental and emotional

Table 8.1: Percentage of Staff in English and German Comprehensive
Schools Identifying Stress Reactions

Stress Reactions	English	German
Irritability	55	54
The loss of a sense of humour	36	28
Increased aggressiveness	17	13
Moodiness	32	34
The inability to make decisions	14	10
Accident proneness	5	2
Feverish activity with little purpose	33	12
Inability to concentrate	30	42
Frequent use of tranquillisers	7	2
Absenteeism	3	1
Marital or family conflict	23	12
Insomnia	21	12
Increased drinking	8	2
Ulcers	7	10
Depression	50	32
Frequent forgetfulness	30	28
Tension headaches	37	28
Skin rash	9	5
Inability to eat	4	3
Hyper-sensitive to criticism	32	30
Increased smoking	15	16
Back pain	7	13
Migraine	9	5
Apathy	26	30

reactions to the closure of a school were obtained by interviewing staff
and recording their statements during group discussions. But I also use
check lists in my action research and these results will now be discussed.

My first check list was used in an investigation of staff stress in two
English and two West German comprehensive schools (Dunham 1980a).
The teachers completed the check list and the results are given in
Table 8.1.

These results indicate considerable staff frustration which was being
expressed as irritability, anger and indirect forms of aggression. Frustration was also possibly associated with depression and apathy. A second
major emotional response was anxiety, which was expressed as high
levels of physical and mental activity which in some cases were unproductive, in the sense that the teachers' skills were impaired because
of poor concentration and the inability to remember important information. Staff stress in these schools was also probably related to the
development of psychosomatic symptoms which included stomach

Table 8.2: Percentage of Staff in Three English Comprehensive Schools Identifying Stress Reactions

Stress Reactions	Schools		
	A	B	C
1. Large increase in consumption of alcohol	0	10	3
2. Marital or family conflict	3	5	14
3. The marked reduction of contacts with people outside school	36	22	35
4. Displaced aggression — displacement on to children or colleagues or people outside school	20	18	14
5. Apathy	25	18	14
6. Wanting to leave teaching	25	15	20
7. Unwilling to support colleagues	0	0	3
8. Strong feelings of being unable to cope	7	16	8
9. Irritability	18	34	24
10. Moodiness	7	19	22
11. Inability to make decisions	0	4	6
12. Feverish activity with little purpose	7	18	10
13. Inability to concentrate	14	8	10
14. Absenteeism	0	0	3
15. Depression	3	11	8
16. Tension headaches	14	15	18
17. Feelings of exhaustion	36	46	41
18. Frustration because there was little sense of achievement	32	30	16
19. Withdrawal from staff contact	14	7	14
20. Anger	7	11	12
21. Anxiety	3	23	16
22. Loss of sleep	14	15	14
23. Loss of weight	0	5	0
24. Feelings of isolation in school	10	8	11
25. Feelings of fear	0	8	3
26. Feelings of guilt	7	10	9
27. Over-eating	14	15	14
28. Skin-rash	3	5	0
29. Large increase in smoking	0	4	9
30. Hyper-sensitivity to criticism	7	11	18
31. Back pain	7	8	7
32. Any other			

upsets, pain and skin disorders.

My current check list has been used in 1982 and 1983 in three comprehensive schools which had invited me to work with them in staff development conferences. The teachers were asked to indicate which reactions they had experienced in the present school year and a rough assessment of their frequency was sought by asking them to identify which they had experienced very often, often, sometimes or rarely. The information from these surveys, given in Table 8.2, is restricted to the percentage of teachers who identified each reaction very often or often.

The 'Any Other' item identified several reactions which were not on my check list. These were feelings of tearfulness, need for increased sleep, loss of self-confidence, palpitations, asthma, reduction in sex life, muscular pains in shoulders, worry, indigestion, erratic work habits, restlessness, resentment, look for someone to blame, disappointment, lethargy, occasional bouts of hand-shaking, many aches and pains (particularly neck and legs), fear of failure, loss of sex drive, high blood pressure, arrive home like wet rag, deterioration in self-esteem and feeling numb.

The check list results again indicate high levels of frustration which were expressed as irritability, displaced aggression, moodiness, tension headaches, apathy and wanting to leave teaching. Anxiety was frequently experienced by the staff of two schools and it was probably related to loss of sleep, over-eating and poor concentration. The highest levels of reported stress reactions were feelings of exhaustion, the marked reduction of contacts with people outside school and withdrawal from staff contact inside school.

The use of the check lists to obtain information about staff reactions to occupational pressures has several disadvantages. The items on the list, e.g. depression, are probably understood differently by the people who read them. They may be reluctant to accept that they have some of these problems, e.g. marital or family conflict. They may also have conflicting definitions of very often or often. When I used this check list in preparation for the staff development conferences in the three schools there was a minority of the staff who did not complete them so my results do not indicate the stress reactions of *all* teachers.

Stress Reactions of Senior and Middle Management

My research methods, therefore, include the use of more open-ended interviews and questionnaires in which staff can give as much information as they want me to have. The results from these methods will now be used to give details of the stress reactions of senior and middle management.

Heads of Department have reported frustration, anxiety and physical symptoms. Their frustration was expressed in different ways but the severity of some of their reactions is indicated in the following statements:

(i) Complete frustration which one fears might lead to indifference.

(ii) A constant sense of frustration, which in turn can lead to demoralisation, when the difficulties become exaggerated.

(iii) Frustration which leads to a withdrawal from responsibility.

(iv) My own particular stress arises in part from a sense of frustration at being unable to move upwards from my present position owing to my having reached the age of 50, which seems to be regarded unfavourably for promotion to 'higher management'. Although I enjoy my present work, therefore, I am now and then struck by a sense of being trapped; a form of depression, I suppose. I mention this because I believe it to be very widespread in 'middle management' teachers of my age. (Indeed a close colleague in similar circumstances recently suffered a complete breakdown — fortunately he is now recovered.) There is of course, no answer to this problem.

These Heads of Department also identified anxiety and two statements illustrate this reaction:

I feel insecure when I am unsure of my role definitions and when I feel threatened; I find myself getting very tense and anxious and I am always pushed for time and I have to make myself relax.

Physical symptoms were also reported:

I get very tired towards the end of the term; I suffer from psychosomatic symptoms and sickness.

One Head of Department identified his stress reactions as a sequence of emotional and physical symptoms through the school year. This process was in three stages:

At the Beginning of the Year
Anger, frustration and a desire to do battle.
Midway Through the Year
Frustration, weakness and a number of minor ailments.
Towards the End
Utter exhaustion.

The members of senior management teams have reported severe emotional, behavioural, mental and psychosomatic symptoms. My information about the reactions of Deputy Heads in secondary schools has come from small groups of Deputies and from a conference of all the Deputies in one LEA. Their reactions included:

> From mild frustration via irritability to resignation; occasional exhaustion; one is compelled to feel inefficient; fatigue; absorption; anger; frustration; doing everything in a hurry; reaction sets in later with tremendous tiredness; annoyance; disappointment; high blood pressure; depression; frustration followed by apathy; work longer and longer hours; one just hangs on and hopes.

Some understanding of what these reactions meant to individual Deputies may be gained from the following three reports:

(1) In highly stressful situations I am unable to switch myself off from the situation and there is much brooding and tension. I attempt to forget about it after work but it can colour a whole holiday if it is left unresolved. I absorb myself in mental tasks, reading, computer programming, and I know I don't get enough physical exercise! My physical symptoms are headache, fatigue and a loss of motivation.

(2) I become stiff and cannot relax, very irritable, withdrawn and distant and I get headaches.

(3) The normal feelings of frustration result in questioning whether the battle is worthwhile. On the occasions when I've decided it isn't, the feelings of anxiety and guilt loom large because the difficulties were not faced. Often there is anger with myself at not being able to cope as well as I had wished. Psychosomatically my responses are common enough — headaches, backache, chest tightness, difficulty with breathing. At their most frightening the reactions are feelings of numbness, loss of contact and inability to make decisions.

These manifestations of stress are also found in Headteachers' reports of their reactions to the pressures they experience in school:

Emotional Reactions

My responses to any stress situations are nearly all of the frustration type as the solutions to the individual problems are beyond my ultimate control. My role as Head is simply to keep on bringing these matters to the attention of County until something is done. The staleness and fatigue experienced as term reaches about its ninth week are inevitable.

I retain a feeling of anxiety. This leads to sleepless nights and a general feeling of depression; I react very strongly with a mixture of intense anger and anxiety.

Mental Disturbance

My response to a 'stress situation' is to go into 'overdrive', to talk more quickly than ever and to make rapid decisions which makes it difficult for colleagues to keep pace. This, of course, leads to further stress as it does not lead to successful problem solving.

Patches of memory disappear — I forget my secretary's name or stop in mid-sentence searching for a very ordinary word. I sometimes have no idea what I did the day before. Small decisions or tasks loom menacingly like giants.

Behavioural Signs of Stress

Stress causes me actively to avoid people.

Physical Reactions

Any big meeting is stressful. I go round like a bear with a sore head before it, and get starving hungry and very tired immediately after it.

Under heavy stress I get physical reactions, i.e. upset stomach and tension in the neck and shoulders area.

These physical, behavioural, mental and emotional indicators of stress show a wide range of reactions to occupational pressures. It is, therefore, important to offset this perspective by noting that some teachers have reported that they can handle heavy demands in school without experiencing any of these signs of stress. If their coping strategies can be identified and then shared with colleagues suffering from stress reactions a good start will have been made towards stress reduction and prevention. The next chapter is, therefore, concerned with the resources which teachers use to reduce stress.

9 THE IDENTIFICATION OF TEACHERS' COPING RESOURCES

In the last chapter I concluded that continual exposure to the circumstances identified in the previous chapters of this book were responsible for the development of a sequence of behavioural, emotional, mental and physical reactions if they were significantly greater than teachers' coping resources. But my research has also revealed considerable differences between teachers in their responses to similar experiences in school; for example, during reorganisation and other major changes some teachers reported few signs of adverse reactions and gave several indications of positive responses such as an increased zest in their teaching. These results directed my attention to the strategies teachers use when they encounter heavy work pressures. I found that they were using a broad range of resources which I shall identify in this chapter as personal, interpersonal, organisational and community.

This perspective of coping resources is very similar to a number of approaches which have been made towards understanding how people cope with adversities without developing major stress reactions. In a study published 20 years ago, Caplan (1964) identified the seven characteristics of coping behaviour as:

1. Active search for information.
2. Free expression of both positive and negative feelings.
3. Asking for help from other people.
4. Breaking problems down into manageable bits and working through them one at a time.
5. Countering fatigue by pacing one's efforts.
6. Active mastery of feelings where possible but acceptance of lack of control when it occurs.
7. Trust in oneself and optimism about outcome.

A study by Mechanic (1967) published three years later proposed that when people attempt to cope with heavy pressures they bring into operation skills, experience, knowledge and personality characteristics in addition to supportive relationships at work, at home and in the community. This perspective suggests that in attempting to understand stress reactions more attention should be given to problem solving and coping behaviour. The writer argued:

> If we are to understand the stress situation of a man falling out of a boat, the main determinant of how much stress he experiences will be whether or not he can swim.

He argued that the extent to which a person experiences stress in any situation depends on the manner in which he assesses both the demands and his competence in dealing with them, and in his preparation of the skills necessary for him to handle these demands with a greater sense of competence.

A third perspective on coping resources, which is similar to the one I use in my work with teachers, suggests that coping has two functions. First, coping is concerned with changing a situation which is stressful. This may be achieved either by altering the nature of the situation itself or by modifying a person's perception of the situation. The second function of coping is to deal with the thoughts, feelings and bodily reactions to stress rather than to attempt to change the stress situation or a person's perception of it.

Both kinds of coping require the use of positive factors which the writer calls 'uplifts'. The ten most frequently used uplifts were: relating well with spouse or lover; relating well with friends; completing a task; feeling healthy; getting enough sleep; eating out; meeting responsibilities; visiting, telephoning or writing to someone; spending time with one's family; having pleasurable activities at home (Lazarus 1981).

This list has interesting similarities with the coping actions identified by teachers in my research and in a study of staff stress in secondary schools in York reported by Kyriacou (1980). In this investigation three different types of resources were identified. The first consisted of talking about problems and feelings to others and seeking support from friends, colleagues and family. The second kind focused on different ways of dealing with the sources of stress. The third type of coping actions was mainly directed towards out-of-school activities which seemed to be aimed at distracting the teachers' attention away from stress at work to more pleasurable and relaxing interests.

Kyriacou also asked the teachers which resources they often used to try and reduce stress. The twenty most frequently used coping actions were:

1. Try to keep things in perspective.
2. Try to avoid confrontations.

3. Try to relax after work.
4. Try to take some immediate action on the basis of your present understanding of the situation.
5. Think objectively about the situation and keep your feelings under control.
6. Stand back and rationalise the situation.
7. Try to nip potential sources of stress in the bud.
8. Try to reassure yourself everything is going to work out all right.
9. Do not let the problem go until you have solved it or reconciled it satisfactorily.
10. Make sure people are aware you are doing your best.
11. Try to forget work when the school day is finished.
12. Try to see the humour of the situation.
13. Consider a range of plans for handling the sources of stress — set priorities.
14. Make a concerted effort to enjoy yourself with some pleasurable activity after work.
15. Try not to worry or think about it.
16. Express your feelings and frustrations to others so that you can think rationally about the problem.
17. Throw yourself into work and work harder and longer.
18. Think of good things in the future.
19. Talk about the situation with someone at work.
20. Express your irritation to colleagues at work just to be able to let off steam.

My attempts to identify the resources which staff are using to reduce stress were based on two methods. I asked them 'How do you try to reduce your work stress?' and I also invited them to identify their coping strategies on a check list. Their answers to this question and the items that were ticked on the check list suggest that they were using a wide range of skills, techniques, knowledge, experience, relationships, thoughts and activities which I have classified as personal, interpersonal, organisational and community resources.

Personal resources included work strategies, positive attitudes and out-of-school activities. Direct attempts to cope alone with stress in school included switching off, trying to come to terms with each stress situation, self-pacing, keeping work and home as separate as possible, bringing feelings and opinions into the open, acceptance of the problem and learning the job in more detail. The out-of-school activities which teachers used as individuals to reduce feelings of tension, anger and agitation included gardening, painting, walking, cooking, baking, cycling, driving their cars fast and praying.

The interpersonal resources which teachers used included talking over stressful incidents with their husband or wife, meeting people who were unconnected with teaching and talking to a friend who had a similar job and using him or her as a sounding board and 'a verbal punching bag'.

Organisational resources came from colleagues in school with whom they were able to discuss their problems, worries and feelings. They also included supportive departmental, pastoral and senior management teams, in-service training and induction courses for probationers and other staff and help from advisers and education officers.

Community activities reported by teachers included bell ringing, squash, badminton, football, drama and choral singing.

The use of some of these resources in the process of coping with stress is very clearly expressed in the following three reports. The first is from a Head of Faculty:

How Do I Cope?
(a) Sometimes the very complexity and difficulty of my work makes it enjoyable. I also enjoy leading a team and exercising responsibility.
(b) I am a very active person, professionally and socially. I can compartmentalise things.
(c) I am a good organiser and within my faculty I have fairly efficient administrative and organisational systems.
(d) I keep many projects, at various stages of completion, 'on the go' at once.
(e) Usually I can motivate others and lead 'charismatically'.
(f) I am fairly lucky in the membership of my Departmental Team who can shift *some* of this workload away from me.
(g) For eight years I practised Martial Arts at a fairly high level, eventually achieving a Black Belt. I occasionally exercise the techniques of restraint and self-control to produce inner and outer calmness that I was taught and picked up in this situation. This is a great help as I tend to remain fairly calm and approachable even under stress.
(h) I am still a keen sportsman, playing soccer at weekends and occasionally training and running in the week. This is a great help in relaxing stored up aggression.

The second analysis of the coping process was written by a Head of Sixth Form:

My ways of relieving stress factors are varied, but within school the satisfactory completion of a major task in itself helps relieve pressure. Also, for myself, the peaceful interaction in teaching a Sixth Form group in my room helps greatly in focusing one's mind and having a chance to enjoy more academic pursuits. At home, I can only fully relax by doing something different, not sitting and thinking about what I haven't done in the day. I need to be active and out enjoying a completely different set of circumstances (mostly away from the people with whom I work).

The third report was written by a Head of Department:

In coping with stress, different things may help at different times. Obviously if it's pressure of work then a 'blitz' may in itself reduce tension. At other times deciding to do nothing connected with work over a weekend can distance school and put things back in perspective. I find it useful to chat through the problems of the day at home — it doesn't matter overmuch if anyone is actually *really* listening. A sympathetic grunt will do! At times I find yoga useful particularly if I'm becoming physically tense as well. Music or a good book can also help. There are times when I find I can positively adopt a 'laid back' attitude and there are times when it just doesn't happen! One of my best general stress relievers sounds very silly! I know that when I come home and greet my husband, a cuddle can make me relax — not great passion, just arms round each other and I can feel tension draining away.

Other coping methods used by teachers can be seen in the following brief statements which are grouped into the four categories of personal, interpersonal, organisational and community. The personal section is sub-divided into three types: work strategies, positive attitudes and out-of-school activities.

Personal Resources

Work Strategies. By working harder — this certainly raises one's self-esteem and not infrequently removes the cause of a stressful situation.
Making a positive effort to be more efficient and organised.

By having at least ½ hour lunch break daily. I used to work straight through.

By making sure that my desk is clear of all tasks I have set myself for the day.

By clearer planning of what has to be done — with specific time allocations.

Having in my mind a clear sense of priorities of what has to be done.

Spreading the workload by listing essential jobs at the beginning of each week.

Positive Attitudes. Recognising the dangers of allowing stress factors to combine in my mind so that I reach hyper-self-critical conclusions: I'm under stress → I can't cope → I can't teach → I'm an inadequate person.

By seeing my problems in the context of the 'great scheme of things'!!

Planning several events, including new and interesting activities, for future weeks or weekends.

Attempting to encourage, within myself, a more confident attitude towards the job.

Thinking positively, i.e. the large majority of pupils are perfectly teachable and the minority which give rise to stressful situations must be viewed in perspective.

Try not to worry about other people's jobs — do your own well and leave others to answer for their decisions.

Out-of-school Activities. Writing — either letters to friends or relations or 'short stories' (sometimes based on personal stresses).

Reading — unconnected with my specialist subject, but useful to my teaching.

Hard physical exercise. Meditation, relaxation techniques and yoga exercises.

Watch TV a lot.

Interpersonal Resources

The importance of good relationships was identified in a number of statements. Several teachers reported that they had decided that their social life outside school which brought them good relationships was equally important to their school life and was not to be impinged upon by school demands.

The significance of interpersonal resources outside school was also indicated by a teacher who was aware of the consequences of not having them:

> If one lives alone as I do then it is not possible to talk over a situation and put it in perspective. One tends to brood and dwell on the problem exaggerating it out of proportion!

The support that teachers received from wife or husband or friends was frequently named as a factor. Four statements can be used to illustrate different aspects of these relationships:

> I reduce stress by talking things through with my husband who isn't in the profession.
> I have a very secure home-life and a wife who understands the demands of teaching and makes home-life relaxing especially when things are harder.
> My supportive relationship with my wife is of enormous help, but not just in providing overt and tacit reassurance but also because of the physical benefits of a loving and satisfying sexual life.
> I am not afraid of discussing my problems or relating my 'horrific' days with a friend outside school.

Organisational Resources

Information from staff which could be classified as organisational resources was considerably less than that which could be identified as personal or interpersonal. Support from senior staff was rarely reported but the importance of good relationships with colleagues was described as a positive factor in tackling stress.

Another organisational factor was the boost felt after attending a supportive course and the resource potential of this experience can be identified in the following three reports. They were written by three members of my course in Staff Management and Human Relations which was held at Bristol University while I was writing this chapter! The first report was from a Head of Department:

> I am writing to tell you how much I enjoyed your course at the School of Education. I feel that it has helped me to put things in perspective. It takes an effort to analyse situations but your course has made me feel it to be a worthwhile exercise.

The second report was written by a Head of Year:

> I'd like to thank you for organising and leading the course last week. It was stimulating, useful and practical. Of course the practice is

quite hard and I certainly felt a 'low' on Monday when the daily grind, with all its pressures reasserted itself. However I have notes to look back on and I am 'forcing' myself to keep these on *top* of the desk. I will be giving a report to the Head later this week and hope to disseminate the ideas to the staff development group soon. I do hope that a further course will be organised and I hope that we shall meet again in the near future.

The third report on my course was written by a Head of House:

I enjoyed last week's 'stress' course so much that I thought a written note appropriate. Many thanks for organising such a stimulating course! I hope the follow-up course can be successfully organised. I have written a report for my headmaster and he responded to it with interest and enthusiasm. I will be trying to innovate and pass on some of the key points from the course with my colleagues. Depending on my successes or failures this may provide some issues to be included in the follow-up course. If so I will be in touch. If I can help in any other way please let me know.

Community Resources

The community activities which teachers reported — for example football, gliding and sailing — seemed to have for some of them an importance beyond that of relaxation or pleasure. The activities seem to have enabled them to assume life styles which were alternatives to those followed in their professional roles. Their importance was indicated by a teacher who wrote:

I am fully involved in local politics and gain enormous satisfaction from it.

This strategy of having activities which have nothing to do with teaching was frequently associated with another tactic — which was having nothing to do with teachers outside school. A teacher in a secondary school described these two methods of reducing her anxiety:

I reduce pressure within myself by getting involved in outside activities which have nothing to do with teaching and by rarely seeing friends amongst the staff out of school. I suspect the reason I don't arrange social meetings is because deep down I want to forget about work when I'm away from it. I resent this because I would

Table 9.1: Percentage of Staff in Three English Comprehensive Schools Identifying Coping Resources

Coping Resources *How do you try to reduce your work stress?*	Schools		
	A	B	C
Please tick any of these methods you have used this school year			
1. By learning my job in more detail	27	14	31
2. By not going to school	0	2	2
3. Trying to come to terms with each individual situation	50	50	58
4. Acceptance of the problem	72	35	41
5. By talking over stressful situation with my husband/ wife/family	50	46	48
6. By switching off	50	44	43
7. Going on a course	17	2	9
8. By moving away from the situation completely for a time until the stress has been reduced	22	12	14
9. Trying to bring my feelings and opinions into the open	50	44	41
10. When away from work trying to make sure that I have a good time wherever I go	22	35	29
11. By involving myself with my family and my own circle of friends when I am not working	47	55	39
12. Trying to think that I am only human and can make mistakes	47	42	29
13. Shutting myself in my office	11	2	0
14. Meeting people who are totally unconnected with teaching	27	33	31
15. I tend to block out work when I get home and refuse to talk about it	5	21	9
16. I try to get out as much as possible on the weekend — going for walks, to the museum, to see a film	17	31	7
17. Forcing myself to take rests before I get tired	22	14	9
18. By talking about it, usually with colleagues at school	27	50	41
19. Trying to say 'No' to unnecessary demands	50	55	33
20. I now admit my limits more easily than when I first became a teacher	27	50	43
21. At home I try to relax by doing something which gives a simple sense of achievement and success e.g. baking, knitting, gardening, etc.	33	34	33
22. By setting aside a certain amount of time during the evenings and at weekends when I refuse to do anything connected with school	55	76	53
23. Any other			

very much like to meet colleagues during holidays, etc. I never watch TV programmes about school — again because I want to forget.

These brief reports of personal, interpersonal, organisational and community resources can now be compared with my second method of enquiry which was the use of a check list of coping strategies (see

Table 9.1).

The ten most frequently used coping strategies from this check list were:

1. By setting aside a certain amount of time during the evenings and at weekends when I refuse to do anything connected with school.
2. Trying to come to terms with each individual situation.
3. By talking over stressful situations with my husband/wife/family.
4. By involving myself with my family and my own circle of friends when I am not working.
5. Trying to say 'No' to unnecessary demands.
6. By switching off.
7. Trying to bring my feelings and opinions into the open.
8. I now admit my limits more easily than when I first became a teacher.
9. Acceptance of the problem.
10. By talking about it, usually with colleagues at school.

On the check list the 'Any other' item was responded to with humour and enthusiasm so I was able to compile a list of additional resources:

Meditation; jogging; relaxation; becoming more detached; listen to music; talk to Deputy and Head; live in small community; let off steam verbally; swimming; dance — where great concentration is needed but of a different quality to that of school work; going out and getting drunk; taking the pressure off by playing squash; making love; develop a sense of humour; seek promotion elsewhere; learning greater self-control; writing poetry; grumbling a lot; if I could afford replacements I would probably smash a lot of china.

The stress-reducing techniques of Headteachers and Deputy Heads were also investigated by asking them the question 'How do you try to reduce or prevent your work stress?' The resources of Deputies included a wide range of work strategies, coping attitudes and organisational support. These methods appear to have replaced to some extent the benefits which their less senior colleagues enjoyed from family, friends and community activities. Some examples of these methods follow.

Personal Resources

Work Strategies. Use of routine tasks to wind down; half hour tidying office — filing — sorting exam number cards; the mind is free and it has an immediate tangible reward of a job completed.

Arranging my office (e.g. putting a bolt on the door) so that I can relax undisturbed for a short while before evening functions.

Coping with the demands means recognising what they are, learning by experience . . . reading professional literature, visiting other schools, trying to keep an open mind, and trying to be objective.

Arriving at school early (8.00 a.m.) to be available before school begins and to plan my day and try and ensure a clear desk by 8.30 a.m.

As I get to know the staff, I know the ones whom I can trust and delegate some of the jobs I used to do myself.

Reappraisal of the efficiency of the ways in which jobs are carried out.

Consider a range of plans for handling sources of stress.

List priorities.

Try to plan my day so that I am available at peak times.

Try to allocate time for all responsibilities.

Have stand-by or fall-back arrangements permanently planned to reduce inconvenience to staff.

I consciously relax body muscles when I notice them becoming tense.

When stress and pressure is at its peak in school, I leave my office and walk around the school grounds on my own. This gets me away from my desk and gives me the opportunity to clear my head; it generally works very well.

Keeping day-to-day routine jobs coped with in good time.

Coming into school when no staff are present to work out strategies.

Have target dates for deeper issues.

Make sure that problems are well defined when you take them to the Headmaster.

Try to be available and to set up routine meetings while the pressure is off.

Investigate problems as soon as possible.

Positive Attitudes. Try to remain calm.

Try to see the humour of the situation — if any can be found!

Accept that many pressures are inevitable and part of the job.

I know that I do my best for all of them.

Think positively — what an interesting and varied job I have!

Accept that some things will not get done.

Accept the situation.

Realise my limits and act within them.

Decide on my own standards for the job rather than those of the Head.

Attempt to discipline myself to doing one thing at a time (not always succeeding).

Try to form a balance between the good and the bad times that are happening. Emphasise good points but deal with bad rather than let them slide.

Keep a sense of perspective at all costs.

I cope by endurance and fortitude.

Develop a façade which permits me to deal with stress without becoming over-emotionally involved.

Resist panic reactions.

I expect to live on adrenalin during the day.

Becoming emotionally and personally detached from the problems.

By being cynical and critical of school and the education service.

Constant self-reminders not to take self and day-to-day crises too seriously.

Out-of-school Activities. A night at home on the headphones and stereo usually works.

Jogging is a great relief in all sorts of ways – also I play squash and work on my allotment.

By having a hot bath and a drink, by talking myself out of my anxiety, by taking my mind off my worries, by sewing and baking.

The cat-nap is a technique I use when the work is approaching midnight.

Switch off outside school and pursue family and hobby interests.

Keep Saturday totally apart from school whatever!

Joining an evening class (Yoga) to make a complete break from school once a week. Also making determined efforts to attend whatever else is happening however tired I feel.

Wind-down on 18 mile plus journey home.

Interpersonal Resources

Making strenuous efforts not to work all the weekend but spend at least one complete day with my family.

Enjoy your own family life.

By trying to get more involved with my own children.

Organisational Resources

I have a very good relationship with colleagues, especially with my immediate, most senior colleagues, which facilitates and makes more effective our mutual support.

Trying to discuss with the Head (this doesn't always work!).

By teamwork and reliance on other colleagues.

Discuss problems with colleagues and involve them.

Finding allies among the staff to try to disseminate my ideas.

Have a good personal relationship with staff.

Persuade staff to use systems correctly.

Teaching is my haven.

Humour is a characteristic of many of our discussions in the senior management team.

Being able to discuss frankly with other senior staff the problems I face.

Have a few colleagues with whom (in different areas of work) it is possible to let off steam and explode in frustration.

I greatly miss the comradeship of my previous school and I regret that, apart from my wife, I feel that I am unable to discuss situations with a colleague.

Talk in relaxed way to people even if (especially when!) uptight.

Eventually, I accept that some things just don't get done and I don't let that worry me — I will even report back to any staff involved saying that 'life was too short'. They accept that because I achieve a lot of 'chasing'.

I unload on the Head and the other Deputy.

Community Resources

Find activities entirely different from school.

Going away every holiday period and half-terms.

Every weekend to have a 'treat' built in — the greater the stress in the week, the greater the 'treat'.

One Deputy expressed his coping actions, thoughts and external sources of uplift as a 'rose' in which he tried to assess the relative strengths of his coping strategies, indicated in the diagram by the length of the thick lines (see p. 113).

The strategies of Headteachers are similar to those identified by their Deputies, though Heads appear to have a wider range of relationships available to them at the organisational level and they seem to be able to make greater use of community activities. The

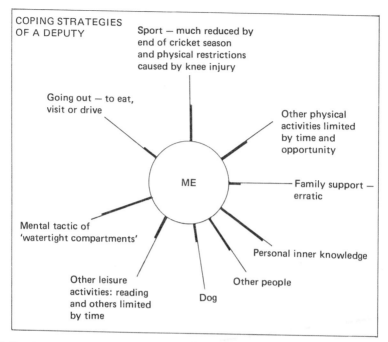

following reports illustrate their attempts to reduce stress.

Personal Resources

Work Strategies. My decision to be firm about boundaries has been particularly helpful to me in coping with stress. I made the decision never to take work home, and to have a set limit to evening and holiday work at school. While this is sometimes more honoured in the letter than the spirit — i.e. I do take inner worries if not paperwork home — I think it has helped.

Positive Attitudes. This particular crisis has confirmed my belief in 'positive thinking'. Although we are all aware of the possibility of closure, none of us have been impressed by the arguments put forward for it. We are all convinced of the justification of our cause and have been prepared to do all in our grasp to secure the School's future.

I am able to relax my mind by planning alternative employment.

I am often kept going by the thought of the next holiday. I'm not sure this is very healthy but the time to recover in the holidays seems vitally necessary to me.

Out-of-school Activities. I practise meditation regularly which produces effortless relaxation (morning and evening). The morning session makes me alert and ready for the day and is a preventive measure against stress building up during the day due to the inner relaxation it produces. In the evening after a hard day's work I am able to totally relax (20 mins) which neutralises any accumulated tension, either muscular or mental, that may be present.

My work stress has been considerably reduced by having a consuming and involving hobby which is cerebral and physical.

Interpersonal Resources

I have become aware of the need for support and supervision, of the value of someone outside the situation who can help one to see the things which are blocked or difficult in a relationship and where I am reacting unconsciously or defensively. I have found some such support through encounter groups, personal relationship courses and more recently through training as a marriage guidance counsellor. I think this has helped me to come to terms with my own stress and worry and to be more able to help others cope with theirs.

Organisational Resources

(i) Staff Support. I feel my stress is greatly reduced by the good relationship between the staff and me. We discuss all problems extensively and very informally, and although obviously the responsibility rests with me, the support of the staff is invaluable to me.

(ii) The Deputy Head. The Deputy Head has a special role as someone whom I see regularly and with whom I can talk openly, trying out alternatives, thinking through possibilities, sharing my doubts or fears and arriving at a decision that I feel is broader based than if I tried to sort it out on my own. Chairmen of governors and advisers can sometimes have this sort of role, but only on special occasions, and then there is so much background they don't know and often they are not available just when you need them. So far I have not had the sort of relationship with a DEO where I could get this sort of help.

(iii) Senior Management Team. My stress has been considerably reduced by the opportunity to discuss with the senior management team the problems in the school. I find that unloading my stress upon them relieves me of my own stress.

(iv) The Governors. There has been considerable support and active interest in the School by the Governors. Also, we are again fortunate

in that there are no personality clashes.

(v) Outside Professional Support. Other Heads and the Advisory Service have provided valuable support in that they are prepared to take the time to listen while I talk out a problem with them. This is sometimes all it takes to solve the particular problem!

(vi) The Pupils. The children have been a surprisingly supportive resource. I made an educational point of involving and informing them (the over-8s) with the developments of the crisis and the resulting comments, work and supportive feelings that have come back have been very encouraging.

(vii) Supportive Conferences and Courses. I am sure that you will be cheered to hear that the staff discussion led by me in this school after I had attended your previous conference in September 1982 has certainly led to a more open exchange amongst the staff here, about the aspects of their teaching which cause stress. The week after your conference I chaired a staff discussion on 'Stress' speaking about the conference and trying honestly to state the stresses I had experienced. Aided no doubt by a glass of sherry, individual members of staff gradually began to admit to a variety of stresses and talked of the ways that these stresses manifested themselves.

After a long and animated discussion we all agreed that there were several causes of stress, but that each of us would cope better if we felt able to discuss them frankly with colleagues, without feeling a sense of failure, but rather expecting and receiving support. I can honestly say that since that meeting, the atmosphere in school has been much better and that we are all less critical and more supportive of each other.

Community Resources

I reduce stress by ensuring that my life is not on a single track. I do this by pursuing other interests — mainly music and sport — so that on Monday mornings my body and spirit are refreshed.

I lead a full life outside school and keep physically fit.

I find that as a member of a motor racing club being at a race meeting blocks out all other thoughts.

As a Chief Observer in the Royal Observer Corps I have different responsibilities towards my crew and this helps to focus attention away from school.

One Head sent me a clearly defined framework of the factors which sustained him as he tackled the pressures of being the Head of a comprehensive school. I would like to use it as a concluding summary to this chapter. In this framework there are five major areas:

(1) *Family life* – I am happy and secure with an understanding wife.
(2) *Job satisfaction* – (a) good pay and a high standard of living; (b) challenge of the job; (c) I enjoy being a Headteacher.
(3) Access to *supportive colleagues* at the same level of Management and also I have the School Management team to whom I can delegate responsibility.
(4) *Leisure activities* – Squash, cricket, music, mountaineering and special short-term interests such as rewiring the house and photography.
(5) *Switching off from work* – (a) by living away from the school community; (b) by mixing with people whose interests are not educational; (c) by having the pleasure of two children.

This list can also be used to provide a link between this chapter and the next. This Head's self-analysis identified a rich store of renewable resources. If the reports from other Heads and teachers are reliable sources of information, his coping potential is stronger than many of his colleagues who cannot find satisfying activities in their communities, nor do they have the support of caring teams in school. They are not able to talk freely with their colleagues because they do not trust them and they possess only a few of the resources identified in this chapter. It is, therefore, realistic to suggest that many teachers need to learn more coping strategies. A wide range of personal, interpersonal, organisational and community attitudes, actions and activities has been discussed in this chapter and the above list provides a sound basis for anyone wanting to learn to deal with work pressures more effectively. But it is possible to add to this store and the next two chapters discuss further recommendations for reducing stress. The first is concerned with methods of strengthening personal and interpersonal resources.

10 RECOMMENDATIONS FOR STRENGTHENING PERSONAL AND INTERPERSONAL RESOURCES

Much has been written about how to cope more effectively with stress. Panaceas have been authoritatively recommended — relaxation, diet, jogging and biofeedback have each been proposed as the definitive method. This single-treatment approach can be noted in a letter I received this week inviting me to speak to a group of Headteachers. The letter concluded:

> One of my colleagues has suggested that you might be able to send us a tape so that we could try out the cure.

Lists of stress-reducing actions have also been published and three examples of these packages will be provided to illustrate the advice which is given in articles and books. The first by Polunin (1980) consists of twenty items:

Reducing Stress
1. Work no more than ten hours daily.
2. Have at least one and a half days each week free from normal work routine.
3. Allow at least half an hour for each meal.
4. Eat slowly and chew well.
5. Cultivate the habit of listening to relaxing music.
6. Practise relaxation and/or meditation at least twice (ideally three times) daily for no less than 15 minutes each time.
7. Actively cultivate the habit of walking, talking and moving at a slower pace.
8. Smile and respond cheerfully whenever meeting anyone.
9. Plan one 'away from it all' holiday each year.
10. Take ten minutes daily (or 20 minutes four times weekly) for physical exercise, some of it preferably outdoors, so you get the added benefit of fresh air and full spectrum light.
11. Examine your eating patterns and balance the diet.
12. If emotional and/or sexual relationships are upsetting you, seek advice.
13. If you're unhappy at work, take stock and look at choices

(retraining, new areas of work, job agencies, etc.).

14. Cultivate a hobby that's creative rather than competitive (gardening, painting, do-it-yourself) and spend time on it.
15. Have a regular massage or join a yoga class.
16. Concentrate on the present, avoiding the tendency to dwell on past events and future uncertainties.
17. Work and act methodically, that is finish one task before starting another.
18. Express your feelings, openly and without antagonism or hostility.
19. Don't accept, or set yourself, unrealistic deadlines. What can't be done one day can wait until the next.
20. Don't rely on drugs, blaming others or other props in order to cope; accept personal responsibility for your life.

The second list compiled by Masidlover (1981) is described as a:

Simple 9-Point Plan to Beat Stress
1. Take the time to relax.
2. Talk out your problems.
3. Plan your tasks so you can easily handle them.
4. Deal with your anger.
5. Get away for a while.
6. Be realistic in your goals.
7. Avoid self-medication.
8. Learn to accept what you can't change.
9. Look after your body.

The third package is organised on the basis of five major themes and has been prepared by the Health Planning Foundation, Arizona, USA:

We work most efficiently under a certain amount of stress. The important thing is to know when it is serving its function and when it is not. When it is no longer serving a positive function, one should try and reduce it by following five suggestions:
1. Spend time alone in:
   a) meditation, or
   b) contemplation, or
   c) relaxation techniques.
2. Do things singly:
   avoid trying to do two or more things simultaneously such as shaving, while eating breakfast, while watching TV.

3. Allow yourself plenty of time:
   whether it be working, eating, talking, listening or playing, allow yourself plenty of time.
4. Learn to spend time enjoying things such as music, reading, hobbies, exercise, and so on.
5. Allow these enjoyment experiences to enhance your life as a whole, providing stimulation and relaxation, rather than considering them to be a waste of time or as a chance to exhibit your superiority.

There is a considerable similarity between these lists and it has been suggested by Kyriacou (1980) that five maxims form the core of the advice given. These are: get things in perspective, analyse yourself and your situation, recognise your limitations, pamper yourself and relax.

One major problem with these packages of advice is that no attempt is made to help people relate their needs to the recommendations. Another difficulty is that there is no suggested framework which can be used for the integration of recommendations into a coherent, individualised stress reduction programme. In my work with teachers in conferences, courses, counselling and now in this book I use the following framework:

Guidelines for Learning How to Reduce Stress

1. The first step is to accept that you are having pressures and reactions which you are not coping with effectively.
2. The second step is to decide that your coping resources can be strengthened. They need to be flexible. A coping skill used successfully in one situation may be unsuccessful in another area or even with the same problem at another time.
3. You will find it helpful to identify your pressures and reactions as separate problems which need to be tackled separately in your stress reduction programme.
4. Your stress reduction training will enable you to develop a wide range of personal, interpersonal, organisational and community resources which you can use to deal with your pressures and reactions.
5. Your stress reduction programme has three phases:
   (a) *Education* — so you can develop a conceptual framework to understand your pressures, reactions and resources.
   (b) *Rehearsal and Application* — learning to use the appropriate coping skills and other resources.

(c) *Feedback and Review* — to evaluate the coping skills which are being used to reduce stress.

(a) Education

The first objective is concerned with the recognition and acceptance that stress is not a form of neurosis, nor a personality weakness, nor an embarrassing state of incompetence. Two reports strongly support my argument about beginning in this way. The first is from a Head of Department:

> The awareness of stress is an important issue. Many people seem unable to recognise the signs in themselves, or feel that they are letting themselves down if they admit to stress. Once we realise that most of us suffer, we will be able to throw aside any lingering feelings of guilt at putting our own feelings first every now and again. Self-sacrifice is an over-rated way of gaining satisfaction from life.

The second report is from a teacher in a school for maladjusted children:

> Pressure is built into the job. I am well supported but I am also subject to pride which at moments of most need tells me, falsely, that to seek help is to show weakness and that if I can't stand the heat I shouldn't be in the kitchen!

These reports suggest the importance of challenging and if necessary changing some beliefs about teaching which may have been held very strongly for a number of years. This process of learning may be slow and painful, but it is essential for the rest of the programme. Now will you please consider the following beliefs. If you have them they will probably hinder your attempts to reduce stress so some rethinking will be necessary. The beliefs are:

1. My job is my life and my life is my job.
2. In my position I must be totally competent, knowledgeable and able to help all the staff (or children). I must always work at my peak level with a lot of energy and enthusiasm.
3. To be able to accomplish my job and for my self-esteem I must

be liked and respected by everyone I work with.
4. Getting any form of negative feedback about my work indicates that there is something wrong in what I am doing.
5. Things must work out the way I want them to.

(b) Rehearsal and Application

When you have started to modify your attitudes to your work you are ready to learn to use a do-it-yourself approach to stress management. One programme based on the work of Meichenbaum (1975) has the following linked phases:

Education Phase — learning to understand the connection between pressures and reactions and the importance of coping resources.

Rehearsal and Application Phase — learning to use new skills and self-coping statements which are used whenever you feel threatened by stress. These statements which offer reassurance and support are concerned with the four aspects of coping. These are: preparing for a major pressure; handling the stress situation; tackling disturbing and frightening reactions; and self congratulations for having coped. Examples of these statements are:

Preparing for a Major Pressure. What is it I have to do? I can develop a plan to deal with it.

Handling the Stress Situation. I can handle the situation one step at a time. I don't think about anxiety — only what I have to do. It is normal to feel anxious now.

Tackling Disturbing and Frightening Reactions. When anxiety comes I will just let it happen. I knew that my anxiety would rise. It will be finished soon. It is not the worst thing that can happen.

Congratulatory Self-statements. I was able to do it. I made more out of the situation than it was worth.

This phase also includes learning and practising new skills and one of the most important will possibly be relaxation. Few of the teachers I work with have taken a course in relaxation training. There are several different methods available, some starting at the feet and working upwards and some working from the scalp downwards. There is no 'best' method. Teachers who are particularly tense in the muscles of their legs and abdomen like to work upwards and those with painful neck and shoulder muscles like to progress down from the head. Four methods are given in some detail so you can practise them and decide which is appropriate for you. The first one starts at the feet:

Relaxation Skills as Personal Resources
Relaxation training involves acquiring skills that can be used to cope with emotional responses in stress situations. The cornerstone of the relaxation programme is the ability to relax deeply and quickly. It will help you cope with stress situations and stress reactions. Once you have mastered the necessary skills you can use the relaxation response to cope with stress as soon as you begin to perceive it. Practise the first relaxation exercises at least twice a day until you master them. At first they will need a practice session of half an hour but soon you will master the skills in a shorter time. Each part of the body is tensed and relaxed in turn from the feet upwards. The procedure for the upper part of the body may be used to illustrate the techniques:

> Press the palms of your hands together and push your finger tips hard to tense your chest and shoulder muscles. Hold the tension for five seconds and let it out halfway for an additional five seconds. Now relax those muscles completely.

Controlled breathing is one of the most important elements of the relaxation programme because you can relax by breathing properly. When your chest is filled hold your breath for about five seconds, then exhale slowly for about ten seconds. Deep muscular relaxation is a skill and so it requires training and practice. When the skill has been achieved you will have the ability to notice relatively small changes in muscular tension and you may become aware for the first time how frequently you have been tense without realising it. Your training and practice will enable you to 'turn off' even intense emotional responses quite rapidly.

The second approach formulated by Murgatroyd and Woolfe (1982) starts at the head:

Relaxation Training Exercises
To practise the routine it is best to lie on the floor or to sit in a position which helps you feel comfortable. Regular practice of this brief routine each day will also aid in the reduction of stress and increase the ability

to cope with stressful situations.

1. Lie down on your back or sit in a chair which supports your back.
2. Close your eyes and try to blot out any sounds. Think only of these instructions.
3. Think about your head. Feel the muscles in your forehead relaxing. Let any creases just drop away. Relax your eyelids. Relax your jaw. Let your tongue fall to the bottom of your mouth. Begin to breathe deeply.
4. Relax your shoulders — let your arms go loose.
5. Relax your neck — let your head roll until you find a comfortable position.
6. Think about your left arm. Tense it then relax it. Tense it again and relax it slowly. Concentrate on it from the shoulder to the tip of your fingers. Let any tension in the arm flow from your fingers. Let this arm become relaxed.
7. Do the same for your right arm.
8. Think about your left leg from the hip to the knee and from the knee to the tip of your toes. Tense your left leg and then relax it. Tense it harder and then relax it as slowly as you can. Let any tension in this leg flow from your toes. Let this leg become relaxed.
9. Do the same for your right leg.
10. Listen now to any sound from within your body — your breathing, your heartbeat, your stomach. Pick one of the sounds and focus on it. Exclude other thoughts from your mind.
11. After about 2-3 minutes slowly open your eyes, sit upright and stretch your arms and legs fully.

The third type of relaxation training also starts at the head. This approach aims at deep relaxation and uses a script which I have recorded and played on many teachers' courses and conferences. I have given tapes to teachers to use at home. The recording is not helpful to every teacher who listens to it because my voice irritates some listeners. Most find the tape helpful and some are so deeply relaxed that they fall asleep! An interesting reaction from two teachers was that they felt embarrassed about using it even privately at home. I am giving you the script so you can prepare your own tape:

Deep Relaxation
This recording will help you learn the skill of deep relaxation, which is so important for stress reduction, stress management and overall health

and well-being . . . sit comfortably, in a relaxed position, and concentrate your mind fully on these instructions . . . take a deep breath, and as you let it out, allow your eyes to fall shut . . . let your body begin to relax and unwind . . . take another deep breath, and as you exhale let it carry all the tension out of your body . . . allow a feeling of peacefulness to descend over you . . . A pleasant, enjoyable sensation of being comfortable and at ease . . . now turn your attention to your body, and begin to pay close attention to the sensations and signals you can detect . . . find the place or the muscle that is most strongly tensed or exerted and allow it to let go of its hold . . . begin to let all your muscles, all over your body, give up their hold and begin to go limp . . . now direct your attention to the top of your head and allow a feeling of relaxation to begin there . . . allow it to spread downwards through your body . . . let the small muscles of your scalp relax . . . let the muscles of your forehead relax . . . devote special attention to your forehead and feel the muscle there giving up its hold . . . feel your eyebrows sagging down and let your eyelids become very heavy . . . let all the muscles around the back and on the sides of your head relax completely . . . imagine that your ears are even drooping under their own weight . . . now let your jaw muscles relax and allow your jaw to drop slightly . . . don't deliberately open or close your jaw, just let it float freely . . . Allow the muscles of your cheeks and lips to relax and grow limp . . . now, all the muscles of your face and head have given up their hold and are very relaxed . . . now, let the muscles of your neck relax slightly, keeping them exerted only enough to hold your head upright and balanced easily in position . . . let your shoulders become heavy and sag downwards as you relax the muscles that come down from the sides of your neck to the shoulders . . . let the feeling of relaxation continue to spread downwards to the muscles of your chest and upper back . . . command these muscles to release their hold . . . you have no need of them for the time being . . . let your shoulder muscles go completely limp, and let your arms rest heavily with your hands in your lap or on your thighs . . . feel your arms growing very heavy . . . relax all the muscles of your forearms, hands and fingers . . . you have no desire whatever to move any single muscle in your entire body . . . pay attention to your breathing for a few seconds, and notice how it has become regular and shallow . . . now let the feeling of deep relaxation spread fully down into your chest, down through the muscles of your back, and down into your arms . . . allow your stomach muscles to relax completely . . . your stomach will probably sag just a bit as the muscles release their hold

. . . relax the muscles of your sides, shoulder blades, and the small of your back . . . let the muscles of your spine relax — the ones on either side of your spine that run from the base of your skull down to the tip of your spine . . . keep them exerted only enough to keep your back in position . . . now relax the large muscles in your thighs . . . let them go completely limp . . . feel all your muscles so relaxed that they begin to feel as though they're turning to jelly . . . your entire body is becoming profoundly relaxed . . . relax the muscles of your buttocks and the muscles underneath your thighs . . . let the muscles of your calves relax . . . be sure to relax the muscles on the front of your lower legs and shin muscles . . . let your ankles feel free and loose . . . now wriggle your toes once or twice and let all the little muscles of your feet give up their hold completely . . . now your whole body is extremely relaxed, and we're going to concentrate on certain areas in order to increase this feeling of profound relaxation even more . . . pay close attention to the sensations in your arms . . . by now, your hands and feet will have become somewhat warm, due to the increased circulation of blood in them . . . tune in to this feeling of slight warmth and allow it to increase . . . don't try to make it happen . . . allow your arms to feel extremely heavy and completely limp . . . feel this growing sensation of warmth spreading out to your fingertips . . . concentrate closely on your hands and arms . . . allow the feeling of pleasant heaviness and warmth to increase by itself . . . simply observe the process and encourage it . . . now, let those same feelings of heaviness and warmth spread through your legs . . . concentrate closely on the sensations in your legs and let them become very, very heavy . . . very heavy and very warm . . . arms and legs becoming so heavy and so warm . . . your entire body is profoundly relaxed, and you feel only a pleasant overall sensation of heaviness, warmth and absolute peace . . . now turn your attention to your breathing, and without interfering with your breathing in any way, simply begin to observe it . . . feel the slow, peaceful rise and fall of your stomach as the breath moves slowly in and slowly out of your body . . . don't try to hurry it up or slow it down . . . just act as a casual observer, taking a curious interest in this slow, steady process . . . imagine you have just discovered this steady rising and falling of your stomach, and you are observing it with curiosity and respect . . . wait patiently for each breath to arrive and notice its passing . . . notice the brief periods of quiet after one breath passes and before the next one arrives . . . now continue to observe this breathing process and begin to count your breaths as they arrive . . . as the first one comes, watch it closely and hear yourself say 'one' . . . wait patiently for the next one and count 'two' . . . continue until you've counted 15 breaths, not allowing any other thoughts to distract you . . . now you are deeply relaxed, and you can return to this peaceful state whenever you want to . . . take a few moments to pay close attention to this relaxed feeling all over your body and memorise it as carefully as you can . . . store the entire feeling of your whole body in your memory, so that later you can retrieve it and relax yourself at will . . . now, before you return to full alertness and activity, take plenty of time to wake up your body and bring it back to its usual level . . . wiggle your fingers and toes . . . shrug your shoulders, move your arms and legs a little bit . . . keeping your eyes closed for a few moments longer, make sure you can sense all parts of your body . . . use your hands to massage your thigh muscles and the muscles in your arms . . . move your head around a little bit . . . now, take a nice, deep breath and allow your body to feel fully alive and flowing with plenty of energy . . . and now open your eyes.

This recording, which uses a script adapted from one prepared for industrial management training by Albrecht (1979), takes about twenty minutes to play and may be too long for school use. For the situations where a brief rest would be helpful I have prepared a much shorter exercise.

Two Minutes Relaxation Skill
Breathe evenly and calmly.
Think about relaxing your body.
Think about tension draining from your feet, legs, body, arms, neck and shoulders.
Notice the tension draining from your body.

These four programmes are just a small sample of methods which are available to achieve relaxation. Yoga exercises and meditation are other possibilities available to teachers. The use of meditation was strongly recommended by the Headteacher of a primary school and many teachers will be interested in his comments:

As a founder member of the British Meditation Society I am very interested in informing headteachers about the use of meditation as an antidote to, and as a preventive measure against, stress. I have taught many practising teachers, including one headmaster, to relax in this way and all find real benefit. Regular introductory talks and courses of instruction in the theory and practice of meditation are available in most parts of the country. The more I meditate the easier it becomes to cope with stress — I find myself staying calm and controlled in situations where it would be very easy to flare up or to become emotionally involved. Many research projects have shown the depth of relaxation obtained through meditation and doctors are increasingly recommending patients to take meditation.

The Head is probably referring to transcendental meditation (TM) which uses a number of exercises to encourage the mind to concentrate on the rhythm of the body and to function in harmony with it. A practitioner of TM attempts to do this in a number of ways, for example by sitting on the floor with a straight back and crossed legs, breathing deeply, concentrating on one thought and excluding all others which may be trying to intrude. The thought, which is called the mantra, focuses on one word which the practitioner thinks over and over again for a period of fifteen to twenty minutes.

(c) Feedback and Review — Evaluation of These New Skills in Reducing Stress

There are several methods of assessing progress in stress reduction as a result of the strengthening of these personal coping resources. One way is to compare your performance on the pressures, stress reactions and coping resources check lists at the beginning of the programme with your results at intervals of about six months. Another method I have used regularly with teachers is an adaptation of a self-assessment technique for business executives who wanted to monitor the effects of 'jet-lag' on themselves. My version is included in full so you can use it:

The AB-BA Decision Making Exercise
Read each sentence below and decide whether it is a true or false description of the letter pair which follows it. If you think the sentence describes the letter pair correctly, put a tick in the first column marked 'true'. If you think the sentence does not give a correct description of the letter pair, put a tick in the second column marked 'false'.

The first two examples have been completed. Check that the ticks are in the correct columns and then complete 3, 4, 5, 6.

TRUE FALSE

1. A follows B — BA   √
2. B precedes A — AB   √
3. A is followed by B — AB
4. B is not followed by A — BA
5. B is preceded by A — BA
6. A does not precede B — BA
(The answers are: 3, 6 are true: 4, 5 are false.)

When you start the main test below, work as quickly as you can. You may well be able to finish in three minutes but whether you finish or not, spend no more than three minutes on it. (Remember you are only concerned to compare your own performance on different occasions.) Start with sentence 1, and work systematically through the test, leaving no blank spaces. Compare your marks at different times of the day or night and on different occasions — such as at the end of a particularly busy week, after a holiday, etc.

It is important to remember that you are not competing with anyone else in this exercise, nor is it an intelligence test. You now have a do-it-yourself kit with which you can examine your powers of concentration and logical thinking under varying conditions. Even if the types of questions you have to ask yourself — and answer correctly — are of a different nature, a satisfactory score on the **AB-BA** test means that you are in good shape to deal with your particular problems.

The Main Test
Decision Making Exercise   TRUE FALSE

1. A is preceded by B — BA

2. A is not followed by B — BA

3. B is preceded by A — BA

4. A is followed by B — AB

5. A does not follow B — AB

6. B is not preceded by A — AB

TRUE FALSE

7. B follows A — **AB**

8. A precedes B — **BA**

9. B does not follow A — **BA**

10. B precedes A — **AB**

11. B is followed by A — **BA**

12. B is not followed by A — **BA**

13. B is preceded by A — **AB**

14. B is followed by A — **AB**

15. B precedes A — **BA**

16. A is not followed by B — **AB**

17. A is followed by B — **BA**

18. B is not preceded by A — **BA**

19. B is followed by A — **AB**

20. A does not follow B — **BA**

21. B does not precede A — **AB**

22. A is preceded by B — **AB**

23. B is not followed by A — **AB**

24. A is not preceded by B — **BA**

25. A follows B — **BA**

26. A is not preceded by B — **AB**

TRUE   FALSE

27. A follows B — AB

28. A does not precede B — AB

29. A does not precede B — AB

30. B is preceded by A — AB

31. B does not precede A — BA

32. A does not precede B — BA

33. A does not follow B — AB

34. A is not followed by B — BA

35. B follows A — BA

36. B is not preceded by A — BA

37. B is preceded by A — BA

38. A is not preceded by B — BA

39. B precedes A — BA

40. B follows A — AB

41. B is followed by A — BA

42. A follows B — AB

43. B does not precede A — BA

44. A does not precede B — BA

45. A is preceded by B — BA

TRUE FALSE

46. B is not followed by A — AB

47. A precedes B — BA

48. B does not follow A — BA

49. A is followed by B — AB

50. B is not preceded by A — AB

51. A does not precede B — AB

52. A follows B — BA

53. A is not followed by B — AB

54. A is not preceded by B — AB

55. A does not follow B — BA

56. A is followed by B — BA

57. B does not follow A — AB

58. B does not precede A — AB

59. B is not followed by A — BA

60. B does not follow A — AB

61. A precedes B — AB

62. A is preceded by B — AB

63. B precedes A — AB

64. B follows A — AB

Answers

1. T	23. T	45. T
2. T	24. F	46. T
3. F	25. T	47. F
4. T	26. T	48. T
5. T	27. F	49. T
6. F	28. F	50. F
7. T	29. F	51. F
8. F	30. T	52. T
9. T	31. F	53. F
10. F	32. T	54. T
11. T	33. T	55. F
12. F	34. T	56. F
13. T	35. F	57. F
14. F	36. T	58. T
15. T	37. F	59. F
16. F	38. F	60. F
17. F	39. T	61. T
18. T	40. T	62. F
19. F	41. T	63. F
20. F	42. F	64. T
21. T	43. F	
22. F	44. T	

These stress reduction programmes, which are based on positive coping attitudes and relaxation skills, might be too passive for some teachers whose feelings of tension, frustration and anger need more active ways of expression outside work. These activities could be directed towards the important aim of becoming and keeping physically fit. They could include any exercise which makes you breathe heavily but does not cause you to get out of breath. This means that these activities — jogging, cycling, fast walking, swimming, etc. — can be continued for long enough to bring pleasure and satisfaction without discomfort. There should be at least one of these exercises each day and you might find you enjoy beginning each day with:

Jack's Six Minute Loosener
(1) Circular arm swinging —
      start with arms at sides of body
      swing backwards and over head stretching arms a little as you
      do

arms down to starting position
repeat 20 times
(2) Repeat by going up on to toes as arms are stretched over head
repeat 20 times
(3) Arms by sides
allow trunk to fall to left side until fingers touch side of knee
resume upright position
repeat 10 times
Now use the same exercise to your right side
repeat 10 times
(4) Arms by sides
turn body to left keeping feet still until you are looking immediately behind you
return to front position
repeat 10 times
Now use the same exercise turning to the right
repeat 10 times
(5) Bend knees keeping them close together with back straight and arms extended forwards — go down as far as you can
come up to a standing position
repeat 20 times
(6) Gentle running on the same spot until you have counted 200.

If you think that exercises are only for physical fitness fanatics you may be reluctant to accept them as important ways of reducing stress, so when you start — start slowly and build up gradually. You will find after a few weeks that you are giving these exercises the same priority as other routine activities such as cleaning the car or housework or shopping.

When you begin to feel the positive effects of your health and fitness programme in terms of increased stamina, suppleness and strength you should consider further improvements. The recommendations of the Health Education Council are helpful:

If no one specific activity appeals to you, that doesn't mean that there is no way you can achieve reasonable fitness. Try walking at every available opportunity. Leave the car at home when you go to the shops. If you take the bus to work get off a couple of stops early. If you work in an office block leave the lift and take the staircase. Climbing stairs is a very good stamina-building activity.

The importance of these suggestions is strongly indicated in the following report of a teacher in a school for maladjusted children:

> I ride a push bike to school. It takes one hour each way which gives me plenty of time to think out strategies to face the day. At the end of the day I leave as soon as possible rather than 're-hash' what has happened because I am totally drained. By the time I arrive home I have usually got back to a balanced state of physical and mental equilibrium.

This analysis of a coping strategy is important for another reason. It provides a persuasive argument for out-of-school activities which balance and are complementary to school actions and experiences and which provide alternative rhythms to the pace of school life. These interests and hobbies have a much wider range than physical fitness exercises. They included those which are manual skills such as gardening, woodwork and house painting, musical activities, creative production and dramatic performances. These balancing activities with their alternative rhythms (Forney *et al.* 1982) can also be found in quite ordinary circumstances which might not be associated with stress reduction — baking bread, polishing a table, scrubbing the kitchen floor and mowing the lawn. There is a need to match high levels of interaction with adults and children in school with low levels of social contact out of school. There is the need to balance the daily hassles of frustrating colleagues and professional communication with supportive friends or relatives and personal talking and listening. Unfortunately there are teachers without close friends or understanding relatives and so, if they want to strengthen their interpersonal resources out of school, they must look elsewhere.

There are several ways of meeting people with whom you can share personal talking and listening. You should look for courses or workshops which are concerned with relationships or counselling or groupwork. These will probably provide opportunities to talk about important personal issues and to express feelings which are tightly controlled in school. Some of these courses are called 'encounter groups' or 'sensitisation workshops' or 'gestalt training sessions' and you should be cautious about joining these groups if this is your first experience of these types of groupwork, because you might be asked to expose your feelings or be exposed to other people's feelings to a depth which is disturbing.

One approach which is usually regarded as helpful is co-counselling.

This method of 'mutual aid for mutual benefit' (Murgatroyd and Woolfe 1982) is based on the idea that people explore their worries, problems and crises. In my courses I use co-counselling techniques and teachers are able to share such feelings as anger and fear in a way that people working together find helpful. The Deputy Head of a secondary school expressed her pleasure at finding a high degree of openness on a recent course:

> I enjoyed the course very much, especially being in an atmosphere in which people felt able to be frank with each other, without this being seen to be threatening.

There are four phases in the co-counselling process:

1. Emotions are hidden and problems are described as external.
2. Emotions are described in a superficial manner almost as if the people do not want to admit to having them.
3. Emotional expression goes deeper and may be disturbing to both people.
4. Understanding and acceptance of feelings as normal which brings a sense of relief.

This process can take a long time or be worked through quite quickly. The pace of development is one which is mutually acceptable to the people who are co-counselling each other.

Another method of meeting someone with whom you can talk openly about personal and professional concerns is to find a confidante. This would be a person who is not a member of the school staff who acts as a sounding board to enable you to develop a broader perspective about your particular worries. You would be able to express your feelings freely and without self-consciousness. This would be an opportunity to talk to someone about your negative feelings about yourself without risk of rebuff, for example that you are in your own estimation a weak teacher and an inadequate person. In this confiding relationship there will be 'trust, effective understanding and ready access' (Brown and Harris 1978). I am the confidante of a few teachers and I have a confiding relationship outside my family with several people and I gain much support from it. Hopefully your school will have a list of people who could be contacted to see if they would be prepared to meet you occasionally. If you cannot get help in this way follow my suggestion of joining a relationships, counselling or groupwork course.

The course tutor or a group member should be able to help you.

These recommendations for strengthening interpersonal and personal resources might be perceived as merely palliative and peripheral in their contributions to the reduction of stress in teaching. Teachers who make these criticisms ask for 'direct-action' recommendations to help them develop school-based strategies and actions. These recommendations are examined in the next chapter which is concerned with the strengthening of organisational resources.

11 RECOMMENDATIONS FOR STRENGTHENING ORGANISATIONAL RESOURCES

Teachers have made many recommendations for the improvement of the management and administrative systems of their schools and of the services provided by their LEAs. Their main proposals were: effective selection procedures; induction programmes for all staff; the expansion of staff development opportunities and more support from their colleagues and LEA staff. These items will, therefore, provide the frame of reference for my discussion in this chapter of the actions to be taken to strengthen organisational resources. The first concern to be considered is the improvement of staff selection.

Effective Selection Procedures

Mistakes in appointing staff will probably never be totally eliminated but the chances of appointing an unsuitable Head or teacher can be reduced by following a systematic selection process in which each of the stages in the process is recognised to be significant in determining the final decision. These interdependent stages are:

1. Analysis of the tasks performed by the post holder leading to the preparation of the job description.
2. Analysis of the personality, qualifications, training and experience of the person most likely to meet the requirements of the post, i.e. the person specification.
3. Preparation of the advertisement which should be a brief summary of the job description and person specification. The complete description and specification should be sent to enquirers about the post. In this way some self-guidance takes place if some teachers decide that the post is not suitable for them. This makes the next stage more manageable.
4. Longlisting and shortlisting now take place using information supplied by the candidates and their referees. A structured questionnaire should be used for taking up references based on the job description and person specification which should also be sent to the referees.

137

5. Interviewing in which all the people involved (interviewers and interviewees) are well prepared for their respective contributions.
6. Decision making in relation to the job description and person specification rather than a comparison of the candidates. Disappointed external candidates are grateful for feedback on the reasons for their non-appointment and on their interviewing style. The internal candidates who are not appointed need more than one post-interview session to cope effectively and productively with their disappointment.
7. Analysis of the interviews by the interviewers and possibly by the interviewees.
8. Follow-up of the person appointed by having regular review interviews using the job description as the initial framework.

If these eight steps are integrated into a school's selection programme the three conditions which are essential for the improvement of selection and interviewing skills will be fulfilled. These three vital requirements are:

1. Interviewers should know how to prepare a job description.
2. Interviewers should know how to assess the key factors in the candidates by the use of a systematic interview.
3. Interviewers should be aware of the importance of regularly reviewing the effectiveness of their selection procedures.

1. Interviewers Should Know How to Prepare a Job Description

The information from which a job description is prepared can be obtained in several ways. It can be sought in an interview with the person whose departure is causing the vacancy. It can be obtained from discussions with a number of people who are playing roles similar to the one the new person will take in school. In my research with Heads of Department (Dunham 1978) I asked 92 incumbents about their tasks and their replies were used to compile a basic framework of the main tasks of Heads of Department in comprehensive schools. This can be used as a check list of functions which need to be investigated more thoroughly to obtain an accurate assessment of the requirements of a particular Head of Department's post. The check list contains seven functions:

1. Communication with the Head, to achieve an increase in the share of the school's allocation for the department or to conduct

a successful defence of what the department already has.

2. Communicating with other departments or with the pastoral organisation.
3. Communcating with the student teachers and staff in the department either as individuals or in small groups in an attempt to motivate them to work harder, accept changes in teaching methods, reduce their anxiety and frustration, pay attention to the care of equipment and follow the syllabus.
4. Communicating with parents about pupils and teachers (e.g. when a parent complains about a teacher in the department).
5. Curriculum planning, organising and budgeting within the department.
6. Teaching.
7. Staff selection.

Alternative frameworks and specific examples of job descriptions for a Head of Department's appointment are available in a very useful book on departmental management written by Marland and Hill (1981).

2. Interviewers Should Know How to Assess the Key Factors in the Candidates by the Use of a Systematic Interview

The purpose of the interview is not only to confirm what has been written on the application form. The interview should provide an opportunity to amplify this information and to find out about the important but less tangible factors of motivation, attitudes and expectations. These aspects of personality can be explored in a reasonably satisfactory manner if the interviewers pay attention to the main principles of successful interviewing which have been identified by experienced practitioners. These guidelines may be very briefly summarised as the eight points of a satisfactory interview:

1. The chairperson of the interviewing panel clearly introduces the members.
2. The purpose of the interview is stated, e.g. 'The aim of our interview is for us to gain more information about you and to tell you about the school so we can decide if you would be successful and happy working in this environment.'
3. Rapport is established in an atmosphere of informality in a private and comfortable room in which telephone calls and other interruptions are avoided. After the introduction the interviewers begin by discussing an interesting topic from the application form.

4. All questions are asked in a manner which encourages the applicant to talk freely. Questions that evoke a 'yes' or 'no' answer are not helpful. The interviewers should not feel it is necessary to speak if the applicant pauses. The interviewers' silence implies that more information is needed and given time the interviewee usually supplies it.

5. The candidate should be listened to attentively and should not be interrupted.

6. He/she should do most of the talking which occurs in the interview.

7. When the interview is coming to an end, the candidate should be given some indication of future action so that he/she is not left 'hanging in the air' wondering what happens next.

8. As soon as the candidate has left the room the task of evaluating the information should be undertaken. If notes have not been taken a summary of the information should be written into the framework of the job description. When the task of assessing the information has been completed the interviewers should follow my third recommendation for the improvement of selection skills.

3. Interviewers Should be Aware of the Importance of Regularly Reviewing the Usefulness and Limitations of Selection Interviews

They will be able to carry out this interview evaluation if they use a check list of the various aspects of an interview which require attention if it is to be successful. There are a number of questions which are relevant for this purpose:

(a) How well did the interviewers receive the interviewee and put him/her at ease at once?

(b) How successfully did the interviewers open the interview? Did they get down to the important topics quickly? Was the switch (from casual remarks to probing) smooth?

(c) How successful were the interviewers in moving from one topic to another? Did they direct the conversation unobtrusively? Did they prevent the interviewee wasting time? Did the changes of subject seem abrupt?

(d) How successful were the interviewers in closing the interview? Did they close as soon as all the necessary business had been completed? Did the close appear natural and satisfactory to the interviewee? Did it seem abrupt?

The assessment of the interviews and the whole selection process can also include evaluations from the interviewees. An example of how this technique has been used in a secondary school should provide a good indication of its possible value:

> To the candidates for the post of Teacher of History, Scale 1, 21st May 1981
> We are keen to assess, and improve, our interviewing methods at Kent School and would welcome, and be grateful for, your comments on your experience today, in both the formal and informal parts of the day.

Each of the five candidates accepted the Headmaster's invitation and wrote letters commenting on different aspects of the selection process. Their main observations were:

1. The interview was very nerve-racking. I always annoy myself by not verbalising what I want to say very well. Possibly I should ask my tutor for a 'mock' interview and see how I sound to him. I felt very gauche as though all I had to offer was enthusiasm which is not really true. I would have preferred a bit more of 'tell me a little about yourself' instead of launching straight in. The 'pastoral' question sent my heart to my stomach because I made such a mess of it! The interview was not terribly friendly – I got the immediate impression I was not liked and I reacted by being gushing rather than crisp and practical.
2. A good informal part of the day. I enjoyed the opportunity of meeting everyone in the department. I felt more relaxed and less competitive, possibly because the other candidates were so nice and also because it was my second interview.
3. I thought the long morning session was a very positive approach to the interview procedure. Candidates saw the whole school, met a fairly large number of the staff and had lunch with the children and consequently were able to form quite a reasonable overall impression of the school on which to base their decision. It also had a second advantage in that having been in the school for a few hours before the formal interview took place I felt more relaxed during the interview than if I had arrived expecting the interview immediately. The informal attitude of staff having small group 'chats' about the department and syllabus in staff work rooms, or giving information about the school whilst walking round it, were

similarly relaxing.
4. I wished that I had not seen the other candidates, especially when I realised how much more experienced they were than me and basically that I didn't stand a chance!
5. A lovely school — you should be proud of it!

Staff Induction Programmes

There should also be a longer-term evaluation of the effectiveness of the selection process by reviewing the adjustment and progress of the person apppointed. The first appraisal interview should take place not more than three months after the appointment and should be regarded as a vital part of the school's induction programme.

This link is important and if it is weak the advantages of improvements in the selection process may be lost. Strong induction should be regarded as a key organisational resource.

There should be a structured schedule of training for teachers in their first year of service. The responsibility for this induction year should be accepted by a senior member of staff who has received training for the Professional Tutor role. For an effective programme the job description for this important post needs to include the following duties:

(a) Participation in the appointment of probationary teachers.
(b) Provision of general school information together with advance information of the probationary teacher's task.
(c) Counselling and guidance.
(d) Organisation of school-based training programmes.
(e) Arrangements for observing/working with experienced teachers.
(f) Support in the official assessment procedures.

The value of the successful induction course in the development of school-based coping resources can be observed in the following statements written by newly appointed staff in a comprehensive school in response to the question, 'Could you briefly outline what you think you have gained from the induction course which will enable you to function more effectively in your present post?' I was invited to be the external evaluator of the course and I summarised the information given in the questionnaire and presented it to course members at the end of the first term in school. Their answers to the above question indicated that the course had enabled them to:

1. Gain confidence through knowing more about the school and how it functions.
2. Understand how decisions are arrived at in school.
3. Be clear as to who was responsible for what.
4. Understand each Deputy's area of responsibility.
5. Know which staff to approach about a specific problem.
6. Have a working knowledge of the pastoral system.
7. Feel encouraged to make use of information slips, interim reports, etc.
8. Have an increased store of ideas and ways of dealing with children and situations.
9. Have a greater knowledge of what help and advice is available.
10. Have a better idea of what is expected with regard to reports and assessments.
11. Have more understanding of some of the work and responsibility that go towards higher scale posts.
12. Have a better appreciation of how the administrative organisation functions both in theory and practice.
13. Appreciate the complexity of the financial administration in the school.
14. Know the basic history of the school.
15. Have a better idea of the catchment area.
16. Know where to go for assistance and advice about the potential development of my own subject.

In my discussion session with these teachers I suggested that more attention ought to have been given to the pressures which the probationers were experiencing, particularly those that were not expected; their reactions to these pressures; their attempts to reduce work stress; and their recommendations for the reduction and prevention of stress for teachers in their probationary year. These four areas of concern should be an integral part of induction courses and the results of a small action-research project which I conducted with two consecutive years' intake of probationers in one LEA suggest good reasons for this recommendation.

I was asked to discuss stress in teaching with these 70 probationers and they completed a questionnaire to provide material for the discussions. The first question was — 'Which pressures have you experienced in your first term which you did not expect?' Their answers identified a considerable number of difficulties for which they appeared to have had little preparation on their training courses. These 'shocks' included:

Spending so much time commuting between the sites of the school; Teaching classes of remedial children; Having many forms to fill in; Having to do a half-term assessment on every pupil, the need for which has never been explained; The indiscipline of the pupils — their sheer savagery and uncivilised behaviour; Being a first year tutor; Having a large group of mixed CSE/O level pupils; Having a heavy load of work out of school hours; Covering for remedial 4th and 5th year groups in academic subjects — these children have tended to be very difficult; Different attitudes and ideals among staff largely due to age differences; Losing free periods to cover for absent colleagues; Getting to know the rest of the staff and to feel at ease with them; A confrontation with a girl who swore at me in class; Parents' evenings; Trying to persuade 5B pupils to work rather than talk, fool around, etc. — I had not realised how lazy and disinclined to do anything some of them can be; Controlling a large group of mixed ability 1st year children in a combined science scheme intended to utilise a circus type of classroom situation; Different speeds of work within a group and pupils who are very slow and complain that I go too fast; A lot of marking and to keep up to date I have to disregard marking schemes which require normal curve graphs as we were taught at college; I specialised in Biology/ Environmental Science at College but I was appointed to teach Biology and Chemistry — the latter involves a totally new approach which I'm having to learn whilst teaching the kids; High noise levels which make me want to scream; Having to teach 3rd year class of 35 pupils in a classroom with seats for only 30 children; Having a Headmaster who wanders around the school and peers through the classroom windows.

The probationers' reactions to these pressures were similar to those reported by more experienced colleagues, which were discussed in Chapter Eight. Their most frequently identified reactions were: feelings of exhaustion (65 per cent); the marked reduction of contact with people outside work (37 per cent); anxiety (22 per cent); depression and displaced aggression (18 per cent); strong feelings of being unable to cope and loss of sleep (15 per cent).

The statements which were written in the questionnaire give further insight into the needs of some probationers for counselling and guidance:

> I feel a lack of confidence because I do not know why some days are good and some are bad.
>
> I believe my apathy and lack of social contact are related to the fact that I have temporary accommodation and go back to my base at weekends. This nomadic existence makes me moody with the friends I see at weekends.
>
> The depression I feel at weekends is often frightening — particularly when the weekend is so uneventful that I can hardly believe that another week is about to start before I've got over the last one.
>
> I feel much more on edge and more highly strung than usual outside school. In school I tend to be relaxed and confident but when I get home I cannot unwind.
>
> After half-term I did not want to come back to school. I became very depressed and I felt inadequate.
>
> I felt that I appeared inefficient in the eyes of those in authority (Head of Department and Deputy Head) when the cause was out of my control.

These stress reactions were not experienced by all these teachers in their first year of service. It was clear from the third section of my questionnaire which was concerned with the reduction and prevention of stress that they were already using a number of coping strategies. My question was 'How do you try to reduce your work stress?' and the answers were:

1. By trying if possible to avoid over-work particularly when tired.
2. By trying to maintain social contacts outside of school.
3. By trying to learn quickly by mistakes.
4. By talking to colleagues, friends and my wife about things that I am worried about.
5. By trying to think positively (how can I do it better next time) rather than negatively (that was terrible I'd better quit).
6. By not being afraid to ask anybody anything.
7. By getting to know the staff and not just talking to probationers.
8. By having a life outside the job.
9. By not spending too much time on preparation.
10. By not getting to the point where I dislike kids.
11. I do very little as I think given time my difficulties will be sorted

out.

12. I have parents in the teaching profession with whom I can talk problems over and ask advice.
13. With difficulty!
14. In the class I don't battle when I feel I'll snap — I set 'quiet work' which is appropriate, so as to prevent myself getting too uptight. (This isn't often — usually only with very noisy lessons with difficult groups which I feel at that moment I cannot cope with.) It usually works — for them and me.
15. By discussing my feelings as openly as I can with more experienced staff in my department. I feel very grateful that I am able to do this and my knowledge that I am not alone in these feelings helps a great deal.
16. Use relaxation time by being with friends who do not teach.
17. I prefer to do my lesson preparation as early as possible and then relax with knitting or watching a programme on TV before I go to bed. If I work later I find it difficult to sleep because I have work on my mind.
18. Long-term planning.
19. Allocate specific times and days for marking and specific periods for planning.
20. Reduce contact with staff outside school.
21. Going off the school premises at lunchtime.
22. Learn to take things philosophically. I have done this increasingly since the beginning of term.
23. If covering for an absent teacher I always have other work to give the children as the children may not have their books or an essential cupboard may be locked.
24. I appear to be very angry at times to prevent any other child from behaving badly and therefore hopefully preventing any other silly behaviour.
25. Looking forward to Fridays.
26. By continuing to smoke (I had hoped to give it up).
27. By remaining married.
28. Talking problems over with one's contemporaries also helps because they are not in a position to exercise judgements concerning your success in your probationary year.
29. I have cut down my social life, get more sleep and generally take care of myself much more sensibly than when I was a student.
30. I am trying to work out a 'plan of attack' to face the situations in which I feel least adequate, e.g. when confronted by 'cheek'

from pupils.
31. There is reassurance in the knowledge gained in LEA probationers' meetings that one's problems are not unique.

These coping strategies can be grouped into the categories which were used as a framework of resources in Chapter Nine. These were: personal resources, which included coping attitudes, work strategies and out-of-school activities on an individual basis; supportive relationships with family and friends; help from colleagues in school; and community resources.

The final section of the questionnaire was concerned with:

Probationers' Recommendations for the Reduction and Prevention of Stress for Teachers in their First Term

1. A sensible workload – worthwhile but not too heavy.
2. Good communications with other staff – particularly those with whom you work most closely, i.e. departmental colleagues and those who help to administer discipline.
3. A proper introduction to the workings of the school organisation, administration, etc.
4. In my view there should be a teacher in every school whose appointed job is to look after the interests of probationers, particularly during the crucial first few weeks, but also to be on hand at any stage to deal with problems/difficulties confidentially.
5. A specific time when you can see your head of department each week to discuss any problems.
6. The allocation of a minimum number of free periods spread throughout the week in which new teachers cannot be called to cover lessons for absent staff.
7. New teachers should be advised against and if necessary prevented from becoming involved in too many extra-curricular activities.
8. Don't be afraid of asking anybody anything.
9. Get to know the staff and don't just talk to probationers.
10. Have a life outside the job.
11. Don't spend too long on preparation.
12. Don't get to the point where you dislike kids.
13. I think it is important to be able to speak to someone on the staff, preferably to have regular access. One initial difficulty I had was that of finding people to talk to.
14. Out-of-school social and informal meetings to discuss school and

feelings generally with other colleagues especially fellow probationers (we have done this a few times and it really helps).

15. Calm analysis of lessons.
16. Don't bottle up problems.
17. Possibly firmer guidelines on exactly how to deal with children
who misbehave. This not only varies from school to school but
also appears to vary with staff within school.
18. More guidance as to how other people teach, work schemes, tim-
ing, relative importance of topics.
19. Collaboration with teachers running parallel courses on an informal basis.
20. Everybody should write 'Advice to another teacher' as a salutary
reminder to themselves. Here is mine:
    (i)   Try to believe other teachers when they say it will get better.
    (ii) Ask advice from other teachers.
    (iii) Take one evening off in the week and one day at weekends.
    (iv) Don't set too much homework — just enough to salve your
          conscience.
    (v)   You must remember you are not a machine.
21. Have lessons as well prepared as possible with plenty of alternatives up your sleeve should things you planned to do fail.
22. More observation if possible during the first couple of weeks,
more a chance to learn how to discipline a class than how to
teach them.
23. More guidance from Heads of Department.
24. More sympathy from teachers as a whole for the problems faced
by new teachers.
25. More social events arranged by staff.
26. Some advice on how to reduce the teacher's feeling of isolation
and working in a vacuum. Perhaps just by being brave enough to
say how you feel to a sympathetic ear.
27. There should be time in school to watch other teachers.
28. More time to assimilate information about the school instead of
having it hurled at you.

There is also a strong need for a good induction programme for new-
comers at all levels of responsibility. It should include a letter of introduction and welcome written by the appropriate Head of Department,
pastoral team leader or member of the senior management team. The
following letter was written by the Deputy Head of a comprehensive
school and I have included it because it indicates the importance of

induction into the tutor's role:

> Dear . . . .
>
> I look forward to working with you next year and will give you as much help and *support* as possible in carrying out your duties as form tutor. (In this respect I also speak for my assistant.) At some time or other all teachers experience problems: it should *never be* a sign of weakness to seek advice. Form tutoring can be very rewarding but equally demanding. As a family man with a wife and three young children I am well aware, however, of the demands made by commitments outside school.
>
> Your Year Head has already forwarded, or given to you, some suggestions for tutor work, which are intended to form the basis of an induction course for the new entrants, and also material for the remainder of the year. Much of it is self-explanatory, but ample guidance will be provided in the use of the material, at the start of term, and periodically, thereafter. You must, of course, feel free to complement the material with your own ideas.
>
> During the first few days of term it might be helpful for us to meet frequently for *short periods of time* in order to clarify points. Previous experience indicates the benefits of this to new members of staff who, by necessity, must assimilate very rapidly a lot of information about the school and its routines. Established tutors will also be only too pleased to help you settle into the school.
>
> I have enclosed an alphabetical class list (prepared at the end of last term) and also one indicating the pupils' previous schools. On this sheet A (Ex-Good), B (Average), C (Below Av.) refer very 'crudely' to academic ability. There is also some information about remedial help, health factors and musical interest. The information was extracted from Middle School Profiles, but for certain pupils it would be wise to consult their confidential files as soon as possible. More will be said about records on the first day of term.
>
> I look forward to seeing you on the 1st September and take the opportunity to express the hope that you will have a very successful term. Enjoy the remainder of the holiday!
>
> Best wishes

The initial letter should be followed up by sending the minutes of all subsequent departmental and tutors' meetings so that the new teacher begins to get a clearer view of the academic and pastoral aspects of a teacher's role in the school.

The next stage of the induction process is the course for new entrants organised by the professional tutor which will include the probationers. This will enable all the course members to share their growing understanding of the school's aims, organisational structure and systems, e.g. the operation of the disciplinary systems, the methods of pupil and staff appraisal and the organisation of pupil and staff support systems.

The importance of successful adjustment facilitated by a sound induction programme for experienced staff and probationary teachers has been clearly presented by Northamptonshire LEA in its staff development programme:

> The first months or year for a teacher taking up a senior post in a new school can be just as testing and just as worrying as for the new probationer. So much is expected of the person that little, if any, allowance is made for the problems of adjustment to a new school climate, to a new set of procedures, to a new team of colleagues, nor, indeed, to a new pupil population. What we should be concerned with is the organisation's effectiveness and this cannot be severed from the well-being of the individual. The sooner the individual is working to full and effective capacity, the sooner he is achieving satisfaction from doing his work well, then the better for the school and all those in it. There should, therefore, be a carefully thought out programme of induction for every new member of staff.

Staff who have been promoted to senior posts within a school either as internal appointments or new entrants may not have the advantages of an induction course, because of the expectation that they should know how to deal with their problems. This argument is particularly unhelpful in the case of promotion to Deputy Head when previous experience in middle management is unrelated to the demands of the new appointment and there has been no opportunity to take part in a course similar to the one held at Bulmershe College of Higher Education twice each year called 'Preparation for Deputy Headship'. In these circumstances it may be necessary to use a self-regulated induction course. If you are in this situation you might like to consider the following 'Guides of Good Practice' which were formulated in a Deputy Heads' conference arranged by Wiltshire LEA:

1. The Deputy Head should start his new appointment by watching

and listening so that he can gauge the tone of the school. He/she should keep a low profile to begin with.

2. The Deputy Head should be careful not to inherit a long list of trivial jobs which nobody else wants to bother with, e.g. fixing the duplicator.
3. The Deputy Head should press for regular formal and informal meetings with the Headmaster and other Senior Staff.
4. The Deputy Head should quickly establish good relations with the Headteachers or else get out! Disagreements between them should be kept to the privacy of the Head's Office.
5. Headteachers and Deputy Heads should establish complementary roles, building on each other's strengths.
6. Headteachers and Deputy Heads should be seen around the school as much as possible by both staff and pupils. They should also make themselves regularly available in the Staffroom e.g. at lunchtime, for informal chats with colleagues.
7. The Deputy Head should make a strong contribution to establishing an ethos of professionalism within the school.
8. The Deputy Head should work with the Head in promoting staff development.
9. The Deputy Head should foster good links with the community and its representatives.
10. The Deputy Head — as the Head — should have a significant teaching load. When timetabled to teach, then it should be his/her priority to get there and to be left undisturbed.
11. The Headteacher and the Deputy Head should do a fair share of substitution for absent members of staff.
12. Regular meetings with other Deputy Heads at least once a term are essential, as well as visits to other schools.

You will probably make additions or deletions from this list and then establish an order of priority for what you want to achieve in three months, six months and the end of the first year. You may also use your job description to guide you in your decisions about priorities and your self-review of your developing skills and the problems to be tackled next. One Deputy Head on my management course at Bristol University chose to make his three month review in a different manner. His assessment was of the losses and possible gains of his promotion compared with his post of Head of Upper School.

LOSSES	POSSIBLE GAINS
1. Loss of contact with students and associated job satisfaction.	1. Possible replacement by staff contact.
2. Contact with people, and my preoccupation with the time-table and the curriculum may minimise this.	2. Proper curriculum development ought to bring staff contact of a productive nature.
3. My independence as a section head has been lost.	3. The status and influential position of the Deputy Head may offset this.
4. Loss of involvement in General Studies which had an important creative element.	4. My role in the development of the total curriculum is more important but more remote.
5. Moving from my 'safe' status with the staff to a 'dodgy' position on the top corridor has brought more difficult personal relationships.	5. I have a positive enough personality to accept this challenge and I have some staff support!
6. Discipline in the Upper School was my problem but now as Deputy Head everybody else's discipline problems become mine. There is a real possibility that I will become a hatchet man.	6. Somebody has to do it in the interests of the school and staff. A reasoned commonsense approach is still applicable.
7. I was so exhausted by my 6th Form job that I am not fresh enough for this new role.	7. A change is as good as a rest.
8. I have no timetabling experience or qualifications.	8. Get them!

Continuing Staff Development

Preparation for Promotion

These types of self-review need not end with the completion of the first year nor should they be restricted to senior management, for many staff would benefit from clarifying their objectives and assessing their achievements and difficulties.

These benefits are also being offered in a growing number of schools by means of structured staff appraisal programmes which are based on regular interviews with a senior member of staff. One framework for these interviews and appraisals is the teacher's job description, which should be accurate and up to date. These regular reviews provide good opportunities for the satisfaction of important teachers' needs which include: knowing what is expected of them; receiving feedback about how their work is evaluated; being able to discuss their weaknesses objectively and constructively; feeling valued by receiving recognition for effort as well as for achievement; being aware of personal and professional growth.

It is important that the appraisal system is linked to the in-service training provision so that appropriate opportunities are offered for continuing staff development. This linking is particularly significant for those members of staff who, because of contraction of promotion opportunities, are now feeling 'trapped' in their present posts and are frightened that their job prospects may not improve. These career development problems are urgently in need of attention and they were a major concern for the Heads of Department and Pastoral Care Heads on my management courses in 1983. Their specific questions included:

What opportunities are there for staff at this level for horizontal movement say to teacher training, advisory work or teacher centre management? How do we find out about and prepare for these opportunities? What are the prospects for re-entry into the education system if we take a job outside teaching?

These men and women with middle management responsibilities had on average been in teaching about ten years and were in Scale 3 posts. They were very interested in preparing for promotion by improving their skills in writing letters of application and curricula vitae and in being interviewed. They were willing to make available for group discussion, feedback from Headteachers on their interview performance when they had made unsuccessful applications for Deputy Headships. One of the group had asked for a written assessment and as the Head's evaluation contained some recommendations which are relevant to this discussion of interview preparation it is presented here:

I hope that you have recovered from the ordeal of the past two days and the disappointment of not being appointed. The following observations are offered as constructive suggestions:
1. You are tall and obviously find it difficult to find a suitable seated position, consequently you were shuffling around during the interview. All the panel noticed you cross your foot across your knee, which cannot be comfortable for any length of time.

Can I suggest that you sit firmly in your seat, cross your legs and sit with your hands clasped in your lap until you find out what is comfortable for you.

2. I would advise you to relate your answers to the person who has asked the question because it enables good eye contact to be established. I think some of your discomfort resulted from trying to spray your answers at all the panel.

3. Your letter of application was very good, precise and well-ordered. Your list of publications shows that you have obviously been a prodigous writer, but beware, two of the governors wondered how you had found the time to write so many articles and review so many books as well as organise a very large department. You are obviously well read, but I wouldn't try to impress the panel with the names of books and authors that you have used as it makes them feel out of their depth.

4. You are obviously an enthusiastic teacher and you should allow your enthusiasm for the whole school to come through in your answers. You are intelligent and had prepared yourself well for the interview. Your earlier answers were precise and to the point but beware of becoming too anecdotal; towards the end of the hour you were going into such details that you were straying from the point. As a general rule I advise my staff to talk for three minutes, then stop. If the interviewers want to ask further questions they will do so. The role of Deputy Head involves a great deal of personal contact and man management so beware of the depersonalised approach 'I would get them to write a memo . . .', if that's your style with eleven people how can you be seen by 78 staff.

My apologies if I appear too critical, I am certain you are a good Deputy Head candidate and wish you success in the future.

This assessment could be used in several ways, for example in group discussion, role playing and the analysis of practice interviews. I have also written some recommendations for the members of my courses on 'The Skills of Staff Selection' and, as they could provide more material for In-Service Education and Training (INSET), they are given here:

Guide Lines for Interviewees

My purpose is to formulate a few guide lines to help potential interviewees. Whilst 'experienced campaigners' may consider some of the comments trivial, they may be able to make direct use of others.

Interviewees should bear in mind that the interview is a conversation aimed at a particular objective and there must be some give and take between the participants. They should also remember that other factors such as facial expressions, gestures and behaviour can affect the interview as much as, if not more than the questions asked and the answers given.

Types of Interview. Interviewing techniques vary from school to school and it would be extremely difficult to describe the typical interview. It is important, however, to consider the variations which can occur.

Many of the texts on interviewing describe the interview according to the manner in which it is conducted. Thus an interview could range from the 'stress' interview, where the interviewers are provocative even to the point of being deliberately rude, to the 'informal' interview where the interviewer and interviewee enjoy a quiet chat over coffee while relaxing in easy chairs.

Pre-interview Preparation. When an applicant is shortlisted for a post it is essential that he is fully prepared for the coming interview. The candidate must ask himself or herself what the panel will be looking for. Most of this information should be given in the job description; and a careful reading of these details can often reveal more than is at first apparent.

An appraisal of one's own abilities and experience is important, and candidates are advised to keep an accurate copy of the information given on their application form together with a carbon copy of their letter of application. Far too often a candidate is unable to answer questions on a particular topic of which he or she had claimed, in the letter of application, to have had experience. Apart from this, some weeks may elapse after the application has been submitted before the interviews are held. These copies can then become almost essential as memory aids. The candidate who recognises his or her limitations for a particular post is able to bring this out voluntarily rather than have the interviewers do so and is able to make suggestions about overcoming these limitations.

The Interview. Although this section is primarily concerned with the formal interview, it is essential to appreciate that the whole procedure of interviewing begins when the candidate enters the school. The candidate should take the opportunity of looking around the school if this is arranged. This period provides the opportunity of meeting the staff and formulating questions to ask the interviewers. If this informal period includes discussions with the HoD and/or senior staff, then the candidate should use the opportunity of finding out how the department and school are organised and how they function. It must also be remembered that, at this stage, the HoD will begin to form impressions of the candidates as potential members of the department rather than as names on application forms. In these informal sessions, as in the formal interviews, many interviewers are susceptible to the first impressions made by the candidate, who can easily appear to be over-confident or over-anxious. Most panels assume that interviewees are nervous and they will try to put them at ease.

The Questions. Certain standard questions are asked in nearly all interviews; they include:

Why did you apply for this post?
Why do you think you are suited for the post?
If you are appointed to this post, how do you think the work content will differ compared with your present post?

Although the candidate may feel the answers should be obvious, most interviewers expect the candidate's answer to show that there has been serious thought about the post. Because the answers to such questions appear obvious the candidate must ensure that they are answered satisfactorily.

In answering questions candidates tend to show two common failings:

1. They try to assess the question from the panel's point of view and to formulate an answer which they feel the panel would like to hear. Most interviewers are looking for candidates who show that they have thought about their work and who are able to form reasoned opinions. Most interviewers will respect such opinions even if these are contrary to the views they hold themselves. The interviewee must, therefore, give the answer which he thinks to be correct and must support this with an argued case.
2. They are not prepared to be decisive. The candidate who realises that he or she has made an error should acknowledge this. On the other hand it must be recognised that hedging the answer with too many qualifications may lead the panel to decide quite wrongly the candidate

is not able or willing to make decisions. This factor is particularly relevant to senior posts.

If candidates mishear or misunderstand a question they should ask the interviewers to repeat or rephrase it. This practice is quite acceptable. On the other hand if candidates realise that one of their previous answers has been so badly phrased that it could have given the wrong impression, it should be clarified as soon as possible.

Towards the end of the interview, the candidate will usually be given the opportunity to question the panel and to add any information, on topics which have not been covered, which would strengthen the application. The candidate must use this opportunity to the full, if only to clarify any badly answered questions. On the other hand if the candidate has nothing to ask or to add he or she should say so. Asking questions on trivial matters for the sake of asking questions does not leave a good impression. Questions concerning salaries, removal expenses and housing costs are not trivial.

The Internal Candidate. The internal candidate applying for a post meets problems which are peculiar to his special situation, as well as the general ones outlined above. These mainly arise because the candidate will know and be known by one or more members of the interviewing panel. The internal candidate often wonders whether there is a need to be interviewed at all. But the interviewers may expect more from him or her than from an external candidate. It is extremely important for the internal candidate to ensure that it is a good interview, and preparation for this must be sound. It should not be assumed that his 'inside' knowledge will allow any skimping on the preparation. The best method of meeting these problems is to treat the interview as if he or she were an external candidate.

Follow-up. Whether the application has been successful or not the candidate should try to assess his or her performance after each interview. The following questions could be used as criteria:

Did I talk for too long or too short a period?
Did I possess sufficient knowledge to answer the questions in full?
Was I able to answer the questions concisely?
Were my answers to particular questions given in a logical sequence?
Did I really want the job?

These guidelines for interviewees should provide stimulation for discussion and learning and they should be re-written when they do not match your experience. It is also necessary for you to be aware that preparation for promotion means more than learning a few guidelines for being an effective interviewee. It means analysing very carefully the knowledge and skills which are needed for effective performance of the post you will apply for in two years' time. The required knowledge and skills can be acquired in several ways: reading; courses; self-directed staff development in school to gain experience of the activities which are part of the job you want; and to make a realistic appraisal of the pressures experienced by the post holders. If you can obtain the position of personal assistant or deputy to this senior person you will find more opportunities for identifying these demands and the knowledge and skills which are needed to tackle them effectively (Marland 1983).

Preparation for Non-promotion

But helping staff to prepare for non-promotion is also an important task for a staff development programme. The inclusion of this topic will appear negative and defeatist to some teachers but there will be others who will be relieved that this concern has been brought out into the open at last. This issue of the possibility of no further promotion is particularly painful for those teachers who have identified most strongly with the vertical model of personal and professional development. This model equates achievement with promotion and it appears to have been generally accepted by staff in a time of expansion of the Education Service. In the present contraction it is less valid and a horizontal model of personal and professional growth might be more appropriate. This model offers many alternatives to promotion as sources of achievement, job satisfaction and new professional challenges. One alternative can be found in job rotation. An example of this approach is the rotating of responsibilities of the Deputy Heads in a school every two years. Another possibility is exchange between establishments — schools, teachers' centres, colleges, universities and the advisory service are already being used by some LEAs to stimulate this movement. Secondment to see and to work in other schools is a third type of horizontal staff development. Becoming involved in new developments in the curriculum, for instance in the pastoral programme, can bring further expansion to the range of teachers' work.

I have good opportunities for observing these developments in my participation in the training of staff to teach 'Education in Personal

Relationships' courses in Gloucestershire secondary schools. These teachers have reported ten positive aspects of teaching these programmes:

1. It is an aid to revitalisation and the removal of stagnation.
2. It takes you out of your little 'box' in the eyes of the children.
3. There is more rapport with the children because you are showing a greater understanding of their problems and not just teaching a subject.
4. The methods used to teach EPR can be carried over into one's subject area.
5. It is a change not to be on a set syllabus connected with exams.
6. It allows greater self-awareness and self-development for pupils and teachers.
7. EPR helps to create an open and caring ethos in school.
8. Teachers can learn from pupils.
9. It brings cross-curricular teaching which involves meeting new staff and learning new teaching techniques.
10. It is enjoyable to teach because the material used is relevant to the pupils.

This is a good example of the job enlargement schemes which have been used for a number of years in the management of industrial organisations (Cotgrove *et al*. 1971). They have recently started to appear in discussions of educational management as, for instance, in Bone (1983).

Teamwork

Staff development programmes should also be concerned with strengthening organisational resources by helping staff to develop their skills of communication, co-operation and social support. Considerable thought, time and effort should be given to the development of strong teamwork to achieve and maintain departmental and pastoral caring teams. The team meeting is not the only medium by which these aims can be realised but it is an important one. Meetings should be consistently effective by means of good planning, clearly presented aims, good organisation of the interaction between members, well formulated decisions and actions, and follow-up procedures to check the effectiveness of the decisions.

Management training to achieve these goals is now a realistic possibility for every school as there are books, materials and courses available to provide the impetus for INSET. One of the briefest and most helpful statements of administrative guidelines has been provided by Marland and Hill (1981):

Meeting the Needs of Meetings
1. Have as few as possible.
2. Have sufficient.
3. Calendar at least a term in advance.
4. Agenda effectively with few items.
5. Ensure review of and preparation for main aspects in proper cycle.
6. There are three main kinds of meetings: discussion, review and decision; be clear about purpose.
7. Minute rapidly.
8. Circulate agendas and minutes to senior staff as well as departments.
9. Start and end meetings very near indeed to announced timings.
10. Act on decisions rapidly.

When these recommendations are adopted they can be expected to increase staff feelings of satisfaction with meetings, to promote involvement and participation and to improve relationships within the team.

The next stage in the development of teamwork that I am concerned with in my management courses is helping the group members to become more aware of the different kinds of interaction in a team. There are a number of possible approaches to developing greater awareness of group behaviour but I want to give some brief information about the methods I use in management training. The following framework is used by the course members for the analysis of their group's behaviour after group discussions and simulations. Their group leader who has been briefed by me acts as their consultant:

Understanding Group Behaviour
Behaviour in a group can be understood from three points of view. When a member says something, is he primarily trying to get the task accomplished, or is he trying to improve or patch up some relationship among members, or he is primarily meeting some personal need or goal?
What kinds of behaviour can you identify in your group?
1. Task Behaviour. Types of behaviour relevant to the group's achievement of its task:

(a) Proposing tasks or goals; defining a group problem; suggesting a procedure or ideas for solving a problem.

(b) Seeking information or opinions.

(c) Giving information or opinions.

(d) Interpreting ideas or suggestions, clearing up confusions; defining terms; indicating alternatives and issues before the group.

(e) Pulling together related ideas, offering a decision or conclusion for the group to accept or reject.

2. *Maintenance Behaviour.* Types of behaviour relevant to the group's maintenance of good working relationships:

(a) Attempting to reconcile disagreements; reducing tension.

(b) Helping to keep communication channels open; facilitating the participation of others.

(c) Being friendly, warm and responsive to others.

(d) When the team members are involved in conflict offering a compromise.

3. *Self-oriented Behaviour.* Types of emotional behaviour:

The processes described so far deal with the group's attempt to solve the problems of task and maintenance, but there are forces which represent a kind of emotional undercurrent. These underlying issues produce a variety of emotional behaviour.

(a) Leaning on or resisting anyone in the group who represents authority.

(b) Asserting personal dominance, attempting to get own way regardless of others.

(c) Trying to remove the sources of uncomfortable feeling by psychologically leaving the group.

(d) Seeking out one or two supporters and forming a subgroup which provides mutual support.

The awareness of group behaviour which is stimulated by this kind of training is an important stage in the creation of a team which is a source of social support for its members. But before the goal of a caring team can become realistic rather than idealistic, it is necessary for staff to become more sensitive to and more accepting of their colleague's feelings.

In my course this aim of sensitisation and tolerance of colleagues' feelings is tackled by a different form of assessment of their groupwork interaction. The framework for the analysis and sharing of these experiences is one that I adapted from a rating scale used in the training of clergy in management skills (Rudge 1976).

Relationships in Teams

Check the number on the rating scale that corresponds to your evaluation of the team in each of the following categories. For example, if you feel that responsible participation was lacking, check 1; if you feel that responsible participation was present, check 7; if you feel that the responsible participation of the team was somewhere in between, check an appropriate number on the scale.

A. RESPONSIBLE PARTICIPATION   1 2 3 4 5 6 7   was lacking. We served our own needs. We watched from outside the team. We were 'grinding our own axes'

A. RESPONSIBLE PARTICIPATION was present. We were sensitive to the needs of our group. Everyone was 'on the inside' participating

B. LEADERSHIP was   1 2 3 4 5 6 7   dominated by one or more persons

B. LEADERSHIP was shared among the members according to their abilities and insights

C. COMMUNICATION   1 2 3 4 5 6 7   OF IDEAS was poor, we did not listen. We did not understand. Ideas were ignored

C. COMMUNICATION OF IDEAS was good. We listened and understood one another's ideas. Ideas were vigorously presented and acknowledged

D. COMMUNICATION   1 2 3 4 5 6 7   OF FEELINGS was poor. We did not listen and did not understand feelings. No one cared about feelings

D. COMMUNICATION OF FEELINGS was good. We listened and understood and recognised feelings. Feelings were shared and accepted

E. AUTHENTICITY was 1 2 3 4 5 6 7   missing. We were wearing masks. We were being phoney and acting parts. We were hiding our real selves

E. AUTHENTICITY was present. We were revealing our honest selves

F. ACCEPTANCE OF   1 2 3 4 5 6 7   PERSONS was missing. Persons were rejected, ignored or criticised

F. ACCEPTANCE OF PERSONS was an active part of our give-and-take

| G. FREEDOM OF PERSONS was stifled. Conformity was explicitly or implicitly fostered. Persons were not free to express their individuality. They were manipulated | 1 2 3 4 5 6 7 | G. FREEDOM OF PERSONS was enhanced and encouraged. The creativity and individuality of persons was respected |
| H. CLIMATE OF RELATIONSHIP was one of hostility or suspicion or politeness or fear or anxiety or superficiality | 1 2 3 4 5 6 7 | H. CLIMATE OF RELATIONSHIP was one one of mutual trust in which caring for one another was apparent. The atmosphere was friendly and relaxed |

This review of teamwork is conducted by asking each team member to use the rating scale privately and then to compare his or her personal perception with that of the other group members. At this point the discussion often becomes an invigorating sharing of feelings and provides a strong indication of the value of experiential learning.

These methods of promoting the development of caring teams can be used in schools to encourage staff to share their problems, feelings and methods of tackling them in some of their departmental and pastoral meetings.

Social support should not, however, be restricted to colleagues in Departments and Houses or Years. Many members of staff benefit from discussing their problems with an attentive listener. The major benefits are to be able to put stress situations into perspective which enables action to be taken to deal with them and, secondly, to receive reassurance that the difficulties have not been caused by serious personal and professional weaknesses. But staff care should not be limited to crisis management. There are positive aspects which should permeate all relationships in the school organisation. This goal was expressed very clearly by the staff of an English secondary school which I used in my comparison of staff stress in English and German comprehensive schools. Their major recommendation was:

It is very important for teachers to be told how well or not they are working and how valued or not are their ideas and contributions. Constructive criticism is essential provided it is constructive and not destructive. We all need from time to time assurance that we are on the right lines or alternatively sympathetic guiding on to those lines. I suppose if people care enough about what they are doing and enough about the people with whom they have to work then empathy is not difficult. We must have opportunities to express our anxieties and problems without fearing repercussions on our careers (Dunham 1980a).

Social Support

These recommendations for the strengthening of school-based resources agree in several respects with the conclusions of research into the characteristics of healthy organisations. In these studies (Gardell 1971), the healthy physical and social conditions in which people should work have been described and they offer guidelines for the development of healthy schools. Four essential requirements for staff are that they should be able to influence their work situations even if they do not have control over them; their work activities should be meaningful; they should feel a strong sense of belonging to their work groups; and they should be able to satisfy their needs for self-esteem.

Many teachers seem to believe that it is the responsibility of senior management to initiate the support they need. This point of view has many adherents. One of them represented this proposition quite categorically:

Much of the responsibility for improving the social support a teacher receives in school must inevitably rest with the Head . . . It is important that the Head should take the initiative by seeking to find out the problems facing his own senior staff . . . and showing himself to be receptive to their difficulties, thereby setting an example which they would be expected to follow (Kyriacou 1981).

I disagree quite strongly with this belief for a number of reasons: first, because of the severe pressures on the senior management team which I have identified in Chapter Six; second, it implies a one-directional flow of support from the top downwards; and third because it reinforces the expectations of teachers that senior staff will tell them how to cope which increases their vulnerability when support is not available.

My recommended model is different in that it seeks to open up pathways of support in all directions in an organisation — upwards, sideways and downwards. It encourages the sharing of resources between all members of the school community — teachers, non-teaching staff and pupils. It proposes an active policy of participation by all members in the continuing development of a school as a healthy organisation.

Each school should establish its own stress reduction programmes and the following two check lists for organisational development are not meant to be blueprints. But they indicate some of the items which Heads and staff might consider in a systematic approach to stress reduction. The first plan was prepared by the Head of a primary school (see p. 166).

The second schedule was written by the Deputy Head of a comprehensive school (see p. 167).

Stress reduction programmes can also be conducted by departmental and pastoral teams. One project was initiated by a Head of Department after taking part in one of my stress workshops. She wrote the following report six months later for a follow-up session:

Attempts to Reduce Pressure

I have tried quite hard to do something positive here.

(1) *Departmental.* We continue to hold weekly departmental meetings in order to allow views to be shared as well as for the dissemination of information; but now, the Chairmanship, where possible, is rotated, as is the task of taking minutes. Although the former is something of a gesture only (as I have to lead the discussion on almost every topic) I think colleagues feel more involved.

   I have encouraged staff to help/support/advise each other — mainly by remaining silent when others are perfectly happy to proffer suggestions. Last year's two probationers and a third new teacher are in a good position to be really useful here. The settling-in process is more natural, less structured. I find one (male) colleague tricky to handle, however sensitively I approach any issue; where possible I delegate this job to the (male) second in department (sexism?).

(2) *Relationship with Head.* Although I admire and respect the Head enormously, I am unsure of my position here. Where is the line to be drawn between his area of responsibility for

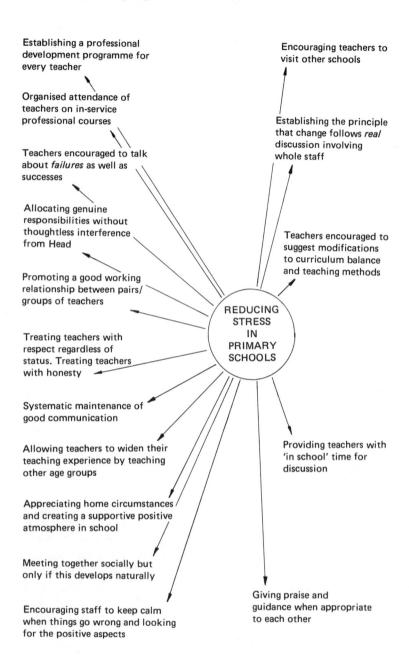

Establishing a professional
development programme for
every teacher

Organised attendance of
teachers on in-service
professional courses

Teachers encouraged to talk
about *failures* as well as
successes

Allocating genuine
responsibilities without
thoughtless interference
from Head

Promoting a good working
relationship between pairs/
groups of teachers

Treating teachers with
respect regardless of
status. Treating teachers
with honesty

Systematic maintenance of
good communication

Allowing teachers to widen their
teaching experience by teaching
other age groups

Appreciating home circumstances
and creating a supportive positive
atmosphere in school

Meeting together socially but
only if this develops naturally

Encouraging staff to keep calm
when things go wrong and looking
for the positive aspects

Encouraging teachers to
visit other schools

Establishing the principle
that change follows *real*
discussion involving
whole staff

Teachers encouraged to
suggest modifications
to curriculum balance
and teaching methods

REDUCING
STRESS
IN
PRIMARY
SCHOOLS

Providing teachers with
'in school' time for
discussion

Giving praise and
guidance when appropriate
to each other

Twenty Ways of Reducing Stress in Secondary Schools

1. Consistent staff support and encouragement, in professional and personal matters
2. Opportunities to talk formally and informally
3. Good communication at all levels
4. Staff involvement and consultation in making decisions
5. Inculcating a relaxed, open and controlled atmosphere
6. Developing an awareness in staff of the problems of other departments
7. Good liaison between pastoral and curricular staff
8. Avoidance of confrontation situations between staff
9. Awareness in senior staff of the individual needs of others
10. Self-awareness in senior staff
11. Developing a shared philosophy and a consistency of attitude and behaviour and decision making
12. Good induction of probationers and all new staff
13. Fair cover system
14. Even distribution of points between curricular and pastoral staff
15. Good domestic arrangements (staff room, coffee, etc.)
16. Efficient timetabling and room arrangements
17. Availability of senior staff
18. Clear role definition for all staff, form tutor, year or house head, department head, etc.
19. Efficient day-to-day routine
20. Flexibility of attitudes of staff

---

the school and mine for the department, e.g. over departmental policy issues? I now tend to seek him out on a regular weekly basis in order to keep him/and me in touch. Mine is a large department with volatile personnel. Whereas last year I would wait until there was a crisis or a problem — now the meetings are less crucial and as a consequence, more helpful (at least, to me).

(3) *Extra Mural.* Much delegation here. Two theatre visits organised by colleagues, one by me. Liaison with feeder and secondary schools is now a shared responsibility.

This report of a stress reduction programme in a department is an indication of the possibility of moving from recommendation to implementation on a small scale within a school. This model of organisational change is now available for other teams in the school to use for their own plans.

The Role of the LEA

Many of the recommendations which have been discussed in this chapter need resources from outside school before they can be implemented. One external factor is support from the LEA and I want to end this chapter by asking that much more consideration be given by officers and Education Committee members to the role of the LEA in strengthening organisational resources. Valuable contributions are made by advisers in arranging teachers' courses in schools and teachers' centres and by providing professional advice for staff. Education officers already give considerable guidance to staff who need reassurance about redeployment or are worried about their careers. But there are further major contributions which could be made and three of them are closely related to the major recommendations in this chapter. First, the improvement of selection procedures by systematic guidance and training of the three selector groups of officers, Education Committee members and governors. Second, the establishment of a careers consultancy service for teachers, advisers and officers which would be serviced by external consultants. Third, the provision of an integrated in-service training service for all LEA staff.

These recommendations provide a brief framework of the organisational resources which could be strengthened by LEA action. Their importance has been persuasively argued by the Head of a primary school:

As a school is a 'labour intensive' organisation, it is imperative that early training is given to aspiring and newly-appointed Heads on, basically, how to handle people. This would include simulation exercises in confrontation. I feel that a lot of a Head's stress is produced by the lack of forethought shown by the LEA in not systematically training all Heads for their posts. Heads can become very insular and besides the Head making a conscious effort to avoid this happening, so should the LEA keep regular, personal contact with the Head and encourage him to express his worries and aspirations and give him the support he so often badly needs.

The need for improvements in the selection of Heads has been con-
clusively demonstrated in the report of the POST Project which was set
up in 1980 to survey the selection of secondary Headteachers in
England and Wales (Morgan 1983). The vital concern of Headteacher
appointments was signified by the officers interviewed by the research
team, but the importance they attributed to the selection process was
not matched by their training and skills. An additional problem was
identified by officers who described themselves as victims of the heavy
demand of local government administration and consequently were
unable to give priority to Heads' appointments. The strengthening of
their coping resources would benefit many officers and help them to
give more time to choosing Heads.

One major approach to helping officers to reduce their stress should,
therefore, consist of practising the skill of time management. This is a
systematic method for deciding what things need to be done, in which
order of priority and how to take less time to do them by combining
some of the items. Time management uses a written list with each item
being given priority rating. Only a few items are given the top priority
and they are tackled when concentration and decision making skills are
at optimum levels. The benefits of the effective utilisation of available
time have been summarised by Albrecht (1979) who has prepared stress
reduction programmes for managers in industry. The points he makes
are equally valid for officers and teachers:

> Most of us always have more things to do than we have time or
> energy for. This means that there will always be things that simply
> won't get done. However, if you make a habit of getting most of
> the valuable, important things done, you need not worry very much
> about the lesser items.
>
> This change in attitude stemming from competence in managing
> time brings a real feeling of peace of mind. The end of a hard day's
> work brings feeling of achievement rather than desperation, and
> those positive feelings make for low-stress living and working.

The importance of changes in attitudes to the management of time
is strongly indicated in the research studies which have been concerned
with the life styles of people who are 'coronary prone'. These so-
called type A individuals are 'aggressively involved in a chronic, in-
cessant struggle to achieve more and more in less and less time' (Friedman and Rosenman 1974). They are ambitious, impatient, highly job
involved to the extent of neglecting all aspects of their life except work,

very competitive and they refuse to recognise factors which are impeding their effectiveness such as fatigue and stress. They also have an increased risk for all forms of cardiovascular disease compared with type B individuals whose life styles are the opposite of the intensive, overdriven type A patterns (Thoresen *et al*. 1981). No research studies have been conducted to identify type A behavioural styles within the Education Service. This will be one of my future projects, because subjective impressions suggest the presence in LEAs and schools of men and women with type A life styles which have destructive effects on their colleagues and families.

These brief indications of the need to strengthen officers' coping resources indicate the importance of developing stress reduction programmes for all workers in the Education Service — officers, advisers and teachers. They should prepare and share learning experiences with the three aims of preparation, support and prevention. Much information has been presented in this book which suggests that with the achievements of these aims, staff will be able to accept present and impending challenges with confidence, competence and effectiveness.

BIBLIOGRAPHY

Albrecht, K. (1979) *Stress and the Manager*, Prentice-Hall, Englewood Cliffs, NJ

Appley, M.H. (1967) 'Invited Commentary' in Appley, M.H. and Trumbull, R. *Psychological Stress*, Appleton Century Crofts, New York

Barrell, G. (1983) 'Knowing the law' in Paisey, A. (ed.), *The Effective Teacher*, Ward Lock Educational, London

Bispham, G.R. (1980) *Initial Report on Antisocial Behaviour in Schools,* Northamptonshire County Council

Blackburn, K. (1983) 'The pastoral head: a developing role', *Pastoral Care in Education*, vol. 1, pp. 18–24

Blackie, P. (1977) 'Not quite proper', *Times Educational Supplement*, 25 November, pp. 20–1

Bone, T. (1983) 'Exercising leadership' in Paisey, A. (ed.), *The Effective Teacher*, Ward Lock Educational, London

Brown, G.W. and Harris, T. (1978) *Social Origins of Depression*, Tavistock, London

Burke, E. and Dunham, J. (1982) 'Identifying stress in language teaching', *Brit. Journ. Language Teaching*, vol. 20, pp. 149–52

Buss, A.H. (1961) *The Psychology of Aggression*, Wiley, New York

Caplan, G. (1964) *Principles of Preventive Psychiatry*, Basic Books, New York

Casey, T. (1976) 'Introduction to NAS/UWT', *Stress in Schools*, NAS/UWT, Hemel Hempstead

Cherniss, G. (1980) *Professional Burnout in Human Service Organizations*, Praeger, New York

Clwyd County Council (1976) *Absenteeism and Disruptive Behaviour*, Clwyd County Council, Mold

Cotgrove, S.F., Dunham, J. and Vamplen, C. (1971) *The Nylon Spinners*, Allen and Unwin, London

Dunham, J. (1976a) 'Stress situations and responses' in NAS/UWT, *Stress in Schools*, NAS/UWT, Hemel Hempstead

—— (1976b) 'The Reduction of Stress' in NAS/UWT, *Stress in Schools*, NAS/UWT, Hemel Hempstead

—— (1978) 'Change and stress in the head of department's role', *Educational Research*, vol. 21, pp. 44–7

—— (1980a) 'An exploratory comparative study of staff stress in English and German comprehensive schools', *Educational Review*, vol. 32, pp. 11–20

—— (1980b) 'The effects of communication difficulties on social workers', *Social Work Today*, vol. 11, pp. 10–12

—— (1981a) 'Resources checklist to help you reduce tension at work', *Social Work Today*, vol. 12, p. 29

—— (1981b) 'Disruptive pupils and teacher stress', *Educational Research*, vol. 23, no. 3, pp. 205–13

—— (1982) 'Stress in schools', *Times Educational Supplement*, 23 July, pp. 18–20

Eysenck, H.J. (1975) *Encyclopedia of Psychology*, vol. 2, Fontana/Collins, London

Forney, D.S., Wallace-Schutzman, F. and Wiggers, T. (1982) 'Burnout among career development professionals: preliminary findings and implications', *The Personnel and Guidance Journal*, March, pp. 435-9

Friedman, M. and Rosenman, R. (1974) *Type A Behaviour and Your Heart*, Fawcett Publications, Greenwich, Connecticut

Galloway, D., Ball, T., Blomfield, D. and Seyd, R. (1982) *Schools and Disruptive Pupils*, Longman, London

Gardell, B. (1971) 'Alienation and mental health in the modern industrial environment' in Levi, L. (ed.), *Society, Stress and Disease*, Oxford University Press, Oxford

Hebb, D. (1972) *Textbook of Psychology*, Saunders, Philadelphia, Pennsylvania

Hinton, M.G. (1974) 'Teaching in large schools', *Headmasters Association Review*, vol. LXXII, no. 220, pp. 17-19

Hoyle, E. (1969) *The Role of the Teacher*, Routledge and Kegan Paul, London

Janis, I. (1971) *Stress and Frustration*, Harcourt Brace Jovanovich, New York

John, D. (1972) 'Going comprehensive: staff roles and relationships as factors in innovation', *Forum*, vol. 15, no. 1, Autumn, pp. 7-9

Kahn, R.L. (1973) 'Conflict, ambiguity and overload: three elements in job stress', *Occupational Mental Health*, vol. 3, no. 1, pp. 191-4

Kahn, R.L., Wolfe, D.M., Quinn, R.P., Snoek, J.D. and Rosenthal, R.A. (1964) *Organisational Stress*, Wiley, New York

Kyriacou, C. (1980) 'Coping actions and organisational stress among school teachers', *Research in Education*, no. 24, pp. 57-61

—— (1981) 'Social support and occupational stress among schoolteachers', *Educational Studies*, vol. 7, no. 1, pp. 55-60

Lancashire County Council (1980) *Active Tutorial Work*, Blackwell, Oxford

Lawrence, J., Steed, D. and Young, P. (1983) 'Monitoring teachers' reports of incidents of disruptive behaviour in two secondary schools: multi-disciplinary research and intervention', *Educational Studies*, vol. 9, no. 2, pp. 451-53

Lazarus, R. (1981) 'Little hassles can be hazardous to health', *Psychology Today*, July, pp. 58-62

Luke, A.C. (1980) 'Communication in education: a case-study of the headteacher's role in the primary school', unpublished MEd thesis, University of Cardiff School of Education

Marland, M. (1971) *Head of Department*, Heinemann, London

—— (1983) 'Preparing for promotion in pastoral care', *Pastoral Care in Education*, vol. 1, no. 1, pp. 24-35

Marland, M. and Hill, S. (1981) *Departmental Management*, Heinemann, London

Masidlover, L. (1981) 'Simple 9-point plan to beat stress', *National Enquirer*, 14 July, p. 53

Mechanic, D. (1967) 'Invited commentary', in Appley, M.H. and Trumbull, R. *Psychological Stress*, Appleton Century Crofts, New York

Meichenbaum, D.H. (1975) 'A self-instructional approach to stress management: a proposal for stress inoculation training' in Spielberger, C.D. and Sarason, I.G., *Stress and Anxiety*, vol. 1, Hemisphere Publishing Company, New York

Morant, R. (1983) 'Developing a personal career' in Paisey, A. (ed.), *The Effective Teacher*, Ward Lock Educational, London

Morgan, C. (1983) *Selection of Heads*, Open University, Milton Keynes

Murgatroyd, S. and Woolfe, R. (1982) *Coping with Crisis*, Harper and Row, London

Northamptonshire LEA (n.d.) *Staff Development Programme for Northamptonshire Schools*, Northamptonshire LEA

Open University E321, Unit 14 (1976) *Role, the Educational Manager and the Individual in the Organisation*, Open University Press, Milton Keynes

Polunin, M. (ed.) (1980) *The Health and Fitness Handbook*, Frances Lincoln/ Windward, New York

Raab, W. (1971) 'Preventive myocardiology − proposals for social action' in Levi, L. (ed.), *Society, Stress and Disease*, vol. 1, Oxford University Press, Oxford

Richardson, E. (1973) *The Teacher, the School and the Task of Management*, Heinemann, London

Rudge, R.F. (1976) *Ministry and Management*, Tavistock, London

Selye, H. (1956) *The Stress of Life*, McGraw-Hill, New York

Simpson, J. (1974) 'The times they are a failin', *Guardian*, 21 May, p. 5

Skynner, A.C.R. (1975) 'An experiment in group consultation with the staff of a comprehensive school', *Group Process*, vol. 66, pp. 99–114

Symonds, C.P. (1947) 'Use and abuse of the term flying stress' in Air Ministry, *Psychological Disorders in Flying Personnel of the Royal Air Force, Investigated During the War 1939-1945*, HMSO, London

Thoresen, C.E., Telch, M.J. and Eagleston, J.R. (1981) 'Approaches to altering the type A behaviour pattern', *Psychosomatics*, vol. 22, no. 6, pp. 472–82

Wiltshire County Council Education Department (1981) *Deputy Headship − Guidelines for Good Practice*, Wiltshire County Council

Woolcott, L. (1983) 'Achieving administrative efficiency' in Paisey, A. (ed.), *The Effective Teacher*, Ward Lock Educational, London

INDEX